C++ Interview Questions

SAPCOOKBOOK.COM

TABLE OF CONTENTS

The C++ Book

SAPCOOKBOOK
Equity Press

☞ QUESTION 1

Calling "getUpdateCount" on a query

What is the behavior of OCCI if "Statement:getUpdateCount" is called after a query has been executed? Is 0 returned? Is an exception thrown?

✍ ANSWER

From the documentation:

"The "Statement:getUpdateCount" returns the number of rows processed so far after 'SELECT' statements. For 'INSERT', 'UPDATE', and 'DELETE' statements, it is the number of rows processed by the most recent statement. The default value is 1."

Therefore, executing a query like "SELECT ename FROM EMP" and printing "getUpdateCount( )" for each row returned would look like this:

ENAME getUpdateCount( )

SMITH	1
ALLEN	2
WARD	3
JONES	4
MARTIN	5
BLAKE	6
CLARK	7

☞ QUESTION 2

VS8: Build Solution Error LNK2019

I have this situation:

----- Build started: Project: HelloWorld, Configuration: Debug Win32 ----- Linking...
HelloWorld.obj : error LNK2019: unresolved external symbol "public: static
class oracle::occi::Environment * __cdecl
oracle::occi::Environment::createEnvironment(enum oracle::occi::Environment::Mode,void *,void * (__cdecl*)(void *,unsigned
int),void * (__cdecl*)(void *,void *,unsigned int),void(__cd ecl*)(void*,void*))"   (?createEnvironment@Environment @occi@oracle@@SAPAV123@W4Mode@123   @PAXP6APA X1I@ZP6APAX11I@ZP6AX11@Z@Z) referenced in function _main
D:\C++ Programming\HelloWorld\Debug\HelloWorld.exe : fatal error
LNK1120: 1 unresolved externals
Build log was saved at "file://d:\C++ Programming\HelloWorld\Debug\BuildLog.htm"
HelloWorld - 2 error(s), 0 warning(s)
========== Build: 0 succeeded, 1 failed, 0 up-to-date, 0 skipped
==========

What is the solution for this?

✎ ANSWER

You probably either missed the OCCI 'library path', or you didn't add 'oraocci10.lib' to the list of linker's input files.

Go to "Tools", then to "Options". On the "Options" dialogue, open "Projects", then to "VC++ Directories". Add the OCCI 'library path' to 'Library Files'

Open your "project" and go to "Project -> Properties". On "Properties" dialogue, open "Linker", then to "Input". Select the "OCCI library" you need (oraocci10.lib / oraocci10d.lib for debug) in 'Additional Dependencies'.

☞ QUESTION 3

OCI-21500 error

I have the following tables:

CREATE TYPE VALUE_TYPE AS VARRAY (8) OF NUMBER (12,0)

CREATE TYPE STATE_TYPE AS VARRAY (8) OF SMALLINT

CREATE TYPE MEASUREMENT AS_OBJECT (VALUE VALUE_TYPE, STATE   STATE_TYPE)

CREATE TYPE MEAS_SLICE AS OBJECT (PERIOD SMALLINT, MEAS_DATE DATE, MEASUREMENTS MEASUREMENT, M_ID SMALLINT)

CREATE TYPE "MEAS_COLLECTION" AS TABLE OF "MEAS_SLICE"

CREATE TYPE METERINGPOINT_TYPE AS OBJECT ("ID" "SMALLINT", "NAME" VARCHAR2(32), "EXT_CODE" VARCHAR2(18), "INTEG_PERIOD" "SMALLINT", "DEST_TYPE" VARCHAR2(9), "MEAS_HDA" "MEAS_COLLECTION", "LAST_HDA_TIME" DATE) NOT FINAL

CREATE TABLE METERING_POINTS OF METERINGPOINT_TYPE (ID NOT NULL, CONSTRAINT MP_PK PRIMARY_KEY("ID"), CONSTRAINT DEST_CONSTR CHECK(DEST_TYPE = 'GLOBAL' or DEST_TYPE = 'LOCAL'), INTEG_PERIOD NOT NULL)

OBJECT IDENTIFIRE IS PRIMARY KEY
NESTED TABLE MEAS_HDA STORE AS MEAS_HDA_NTAB
(
(PRIMARY KEY (NESTED_TABLE_ID, MEAS_DATE,
PERIOD))
ORAGANIZATION INDEX COMPRESS) RETURN AS
LOCATOR

I use 'Oracle9i Enterprise Edition Release 9.2.0.6.0' – Production, with the partitioning, 'OLAP' and 'Oracle Data Mining' options. "JServer Release 9.2.0.6.0" – Production; OCCI client, instant client for linux32-10.2.0.1

I'm using 'OTT' to generate 'C++' classes.

When "MEAS_HDA" was empty all worked fine (Navigational and Associative access). But if I fill "meas_hda" column with data, I get "OCI-21500" [kopuigpfx1], [13]. However, when I tried to pin "METERINGPOINT_TYPE" object ref, the core 'dumped'.

SQL query (For Example, "select meas.*" from "metering_points m", table (m.meas_hda) meas where id = 1) worked fine.

I think it's a bug in 'ORACLE OCCI Client', but I can't find its description in Oracle knowledge base.

What should I do?

✍ Answer

The "RETURN AS LOCATOR" specification for nested tables is not supported by OCCI. You will need to remove this specification from the "MEAS_HDA" nested table attribute.

☞ QUESTION 4

Binding "Boolean" variables

I have PL/SQL function that returns "Boolean" value. I have to call this function in my OCCI code. In the documentation, it is mentioned that we can't use "OCCIBOOL" in "registerOutParameter()" function.

How can I retrieve this "Boolean" value from the output of the PL/SQL function?

✍ ANSWER

Try binding it as an integer. Unfortunately, "BOOLEAN" and "RECORD" types are PL/SQL only data types, and have no mapping outside the PL/SQL context (at least no direct mapping).

☞ QUESTION 5

Setup OCCI Dev Environment

I installed the '10g client' as specified in the 'Client installation guide', and updated the 'Linux OCCI gcc' files to match the '3.2.3 gcc' program.

I wrote a 'hello world' program, and included the 'occi.h' file to see if it would find the 'occi.h' file in the 'rdbms/public' folder, but it didn't.

I included the 'g++' arguments seen on other forum posts:

g++ -o test -L (ORACLE_HOME)/rdbms/public -L (ORACLE_HOME)/lib, -L
(ORACLE_HOME)/rdbms/lib -locci -lclntsh test.cpp

There was no success. It stated that it can't find the 'occi.h' file.

I did not successfully compile the demo programs either, issuing this command:

make -f demo_rdbms.mk occidemos

I got this error:

"no rule to make target. occiblob.o needed by buildocci";

What did I configured incorrectly?

✍ ANSWER

You should include directories that need to be prefixed with "-I", you used "-L" (for library dirs.).

```
CC=
ORA_INCLUDE=-I$(ORACLE_HOME)/rdbms/demo \
-I$(ORACLE_HOME)/rdbms/public \
-I$(ORACLE_HOME)/plsql/public \
-I$(ORACLE_HOME)/network/public

ORA_LIB=-L$(ORACLE_HOME)/lib32/  -L$(ORACLE_HOME)/
rdbms/lib32/ \
-locci -lclntsh -lld -lm `cat /oracle/app/oracle/lib32/sysliblist` -lm
-lpthreads

CPP_INCLUDE=
CPP_FIX =
SOURCEFILENAME=aa.cpp
MIDFILENAME=aa.o
TARGETFILENAME=aa

all:compile

compile:$(SOURCEFILENAME)
$(CC)  -c  $(CPP_FIX)  $(CPP_INCLUDE)  $(ORA_INCLUDE)
$(SOURCEFILENAME)
$(CC)     $(CPP_FIX)     $(CPP_INCLUDE)    -    $(ORA_LIB)
$(MIDFILENAME) -o $(TARGETFILENAME)
```

☞ Question 6

Compiling problem

When I tried to compile my 'C++' program, it throwed the error: "occi.h header file not found".

I checked for the file under "$ORACLE_HOME/public", it was there.

My environments are: Oracle client version: 10g (10.1.0), connecting to: Oracle 9.2.0, Linux version: Red Hat Linux release 7.3, gcc version: gcc-2.96.

Here is how I compiled my program:

```
g++ -o struc -I$ORACLE_HOME/rdbms/demo -l$ORACLE_
HOME/rdbms/public -
      l$ORACLE_HOME/plsql/public   -l$ORACLE_HOME/
network/public -
   L$ORACLE_HOME/lib occi -lclntsh struc.cc
```

What should I do to fix this?

✍ Answer

Check if your command line options are typed correctly.

Here's the corrected compilation command:

```
g++ -o struc -I$ORACLE_HOME/rdbms/demo -I$ORACLE_
HOME/rdbms/public -
      I$ORACLE_HOME/plsql/public   -I$ORACLE_HOME/
```

network/public –
  L$ORACLE_HOME/lib -Iocci -Iclntsh struc.cc

Another suggestion is to keep it simple. You can use the following:
  "rdbms/demo/demo_rdbms.mk
  makefile to build the C++ app".

e.g.: make -f demo_rdbms.mk buildocci EXE=run OBJS=app.
o

☞ QUESTION 7

Calling stored procedure in OCCI

I tried to call a stored procedure in Oracle database server. But I had problems with taking of the 'out' parameters.

Here are the lines that might cause the problem.

```
statement->registerOutParam(2, Type::OCCIINT, sizeof (
if_false ) );
statement->registerOutParam(3, Type::OCCIString, sizeof (
__result ) );
```

I can't access "Type::OCCIINT and Type::OCCIString".
I tried "Type::OCCISTRING", but there was no result.

These are the codes that I used:

```
/* ------------------------------------------------- */
Environment *env = Environment::createEnvironment
( Environment::DEFAULT );
Connection *conn = env->createConnection ( user, pass,
osid );
Statement * statement = conn->createStatement ( query );
ResultSet * result = statement->executeQuery ( query );
result->setCharacterStreamMode ( 2, 10000 );

statement->setSQL ( "BEGIN tracetst.get_tst_moduls ( :1, :2,
:3 ); END:" );
int if_false;
string __result;

statement->setString ( 1, "116714020010" );
```

```
statement->registerOutParam(2, Type::OCCIINT, sizeof ( if_
false ) );
statement->registerOutParam(3, Type::OCCIString, sizeof (
__result ) );
statement->executeUpdate();
if_false = statement->getInt (2);
/* Set the 1,2 args into err_result and modules. The action is
only with these */
err_result = if_false;
__result = statement->getString (3);
cout << if_false;
cout << __result;

//printf ( result );

//statement->executeUpdate ( query );
env->terminateConnection ( conn );
Environment :: terminateEnvironment ( env );
```

/* --- */

While compiling, I got an error message:

```
   trace.cpp: In member function `const char* oracle_io::get_
data()':
   trace.cpp:668: error: `oracle::occi::Type' is not an aggregate
type
```

The next line was the same:

```
   statement->registerOutParam(2, Type::OCCIINT, sizeof (
if_false ) );
   statement->registerOutParam(3, Type::OCCIString, sizeof (
__result ) );
```

How can I call the procedure correctly?

✍ ANSWER

Remove the 'Type' in "registerOutParam". Also, place a semicolon
after 'END' in "setSQL".

```
statement->setSQL ( "BEGIN tracetst.get_tst_moduls ( :1,
:2, :3 ); END;" );
....
stmt->registerOutParam(2, OCCIINT,sizeof(if_false));
    stmt->registerOutParam(3,  OCCISTRING,sizeof(__
result));
```

You should also take note to remove the colon after "END",
to avoid error during execution.

```
...
    Environment *env = Environment::createEnvironment(
Environment::OBJECT);
    Connection *conn = env->createConnection("scott","ti
ger","inst1");
    Statement *stmt;
    int num; string name;
    try
    {
        stmt=conn->createStatement();
        stmt->setSQL ( "BEGIN scott.test ( :1, :2, :3 ); END;"
);
        stmt->setString ( 1, "11" );
        stmt->registerOutParam(2, OCCIINT,sizeof(num));
        stmt->registerOutParam(3, OCCISTRING,sizeof(na
me));
        stmt->execute();
        num=stmt->getInt(2); name=stmt->getString(3);
```

```
        cout<<num><<" "<<name><<endl;
}
catch (SQLException &ex)
{
        env->terminateConnection(conn);
        Environment::terminateEnvironment(env);
        cout<<ex.getMessage();
}
env->terminateConnection(conn);
Environment::terminateEnvironment(env);
```

☞ QUESTION 8

subscription & event handler

How can I implement 'Database Change Notification' using OCCI?

I also need an example.

✍ ANSWER

'Database Change Notification' is currently not supported in OCCI.

As a workaround, you can achieve these using OCI methods within OCCI. You can find a sample program below.

The program uses a subscription handle and associates a 'callback' function with it. A SQL query is registered (to register the objects the query uses). A statement executed would then register the object for change notification.

After execution, the below program would invoke the callback function after an "INSERT/UPDATE" on the registered table (employees in this case).

Check the documentation for more information on 'DB change notification': http://download-west.oracle.com/docs/cd/B19306_01/appdev.102/b14250/oci09adv.htm#sthref1584

Another suggestion is to receive change notification using oracle's 'Advanced Queuing', by first creating queue table, queue, and a trigger that calls "DBMS_AQ.Enqueue()". The OCCI code then merely creates a subscription on the queue and waits from the new insertion event.

Here is an example:

```
#include <occi.h>
#include <iostream>

#define MAXSTRLENGTH 1024

using namespace oracle::occi;
using namespace std;

static int notifications_processed=0;

void    notification_callback(dvoid    *ctx,OCISubscription
*subscrhp,dvoid *payload,
                              ub4              *payl,dvoid
*descriptor,ub4 mode);

void checkerr(OCIError *errhp,sword status);

void    notification_callback(dvoid    *ctx,OCISubscription
*subscrhp,dvoid *payload,
                              ub4              *payl,dvoid
*descriptor,ub4 mode)
{
  dvoid *change_descriptor = descriptor;
  OCIEnv *envhp;
  OCIError *errhp;

  dvoid *elemind = (dvoid *)0;
  OCIColl *table_changes = (OCIColl *)0 ;
  dvoid **table_descp;
```

```
dvoid *table_desc;
ub4 num_rows = 0, table_op,num_tables = 0;
ub2 i, j;
boolean exist;
text *table_name;

//OCCI
Environment *env = Environment :: createEnvironment(En
vironment::OBJECT);
Connection *con = env->createConnection("HR","HR","");
envhp = env->getOCIEnvironment();

checkerr(errhp,OCIHandleAlloc( (dvoid *) envhp, (dvoid
**) &errhp, OCI_HTYPE_ERROR,
          (size_t) 0, (dvoid **) 0));
    checkerr(errhp,OCIAttrGet(change_descriptor,   OCI_
DTYPE_CHDES, &table_changes,
          NULL, OCI_ATTR_CHDES_TABLE_CHANGES,
errhp));

if (table_changes)
    checkerr(errhp,OCICollSize(envhp,  errhp,  (CONST
OCIColl *) table_changes, (sb4 *)&num_tables));
  else
    num_tables =0;

for (i=0; i < num_tables; i++)
{
  OCIColl *row_changes = (OCIColl *)0;
  dvoid **row_descp;
  dvoid  *row_desc;
  text *row_id;
  ub4 rowid_size;
  text *ocistmt;
  OCIDefine *defnp1 = (OCIDefine *)0;
```

```
    char *outstr;

    checkerr(errhp,OCICollGetElem(envhp, errhp, (OCIColl
*) table_changes, i,
                , (dvoid **)&table_descp, &elemind));

    table_desc = *table_descp;

        checkerr(errhp,OCIAttrGet(table_desc,  OCI_DTYPE_
TABLE_CHDES, &table_name,
                    NULL,
                        OCI_ATTR_CHDES_TABLE_NAME,
errhp));

        checkerr(errhp,OCIAttrGet (table_desc,  OCI_DTYPE_
TABLE_CHDES,
                    (dvoid *)&table_op, NULL,
                        OCI_ATTR_CHDES_TABLE_OPFLAGS,
errhp));

    if (table_op & OCI_OPCODE_ALLROWS)
    {
      printf("Full Table Invalidation\n");
      continue;
    }

        checkerr(errhp,OCIAttrGet (table_desc,  OCI_DTYPE_
TABLE_CHDES, &row_changes,
                    NULL, OCI_ATTR_CHDES_TABLE_ROW_
CHANGES, errhp));

    if (row_changes)
      checkerr(errhp,OCICollSize(envhp, errhp, row_changes,
(sb4*)&num_rows));
    else
```

```
num_rows =0;

printf ("Number of rows modified is %d\n", num_rows);
fflush(stdout);

for (j=0; j<num_rows; j++)
{
        OCICollGetElem(envhp, errhp, (OCIColl *) row_
changes,
        j, &#8707;, (void **)&row_descp, &elemind);
    row_desc = *row_descp;

        OCIAttrGet (row_desc, OCI_DTYPE_ROW_CHDES,
(dvoid *)&row_id,
        &rowid_size, OCI_ATTR_CHDES_ROW_ROWID,
errhp);

    printf ("%s table has been modified in row %s \n", table_
name, row_id);
    fflush(stdout);

        ocistmt = (text *)malloc(MAXSTRLENGTH*sizeof(char
));
        sprintf ((char *)ocistmt, "select employee_id from
employees where rowid='%s'", row_id );

    //OCCI
        Statement   *stmt=con->createStatement((char
*)ocistmt);
    ResultSet *rs=stmt->executeQuery();
    while(rs->next()){
        int empid=rs->getInt(1);
            cout<<"Employee ID of affected row is:
"<<empid><<endl;
    }
```

```
   } //loop for rows in table
   } //loop for all affected tables..

   notifications_processed++;

      OCIHandleFree((dvoid  *)  errhp,  (ub4)  OCI_HTYPE_
ERROR);

   env->terminateConnection(con);
   Environment::terminateEnvironment(env);

}

void checkerr(OCIError *errhp,sword status)
{
   text errbuf[512];
   sb4 errcode = 0;
   int retval = 1;

   switch (status)
   {
   case OCI_SUCCESS:
     retval = 0;
     break;
   case OCI_SUCCESS_WITH_INFO:
     (void) printf("Error - OCI_SUCCESS_WITH_INFO\n");
     break;
   case OCI_NEED_DATA:
     (void) printf("Error - OCI_NEED_DATA\n");
     break;
   case OCI_NO_DATA:
     (void) printf("Error - OCI_NODATA\n");
     break;
   case OCI_ERROR:
     (void) OCIErrorGet((dvoid *)errhp, (ub4) 1, (text *) NULL,
```

```
      &errcode,
                  errbuf, (ub4) sizeof(errbuf), OCI_HTYPE_
    ERROR);
      (void) printf("Error - %.*s\n", 512, errbuf);
      break;
    case OCI_INVALID_HANDLE:
      (void) printf("Error - OCI_INVALID_HANDLE\n");
      break;
    case OCI_STILL_EXECUTING:
      (void) printf("Error - OCI_STILL_EXECUTE\n");
      break;
    case OCI_CONTINUE:
      (void) printf("Error - OCI_CONTINUE\n");
      break;
    default:
      break;
    }
}


class dbc
{
  private:
    Environment *env;
    Connection *con;
    Statement *stmt;

  public:
    dbc()
    {
      try{

        env = Environment :: createEnvironment(Environment::
    Mode(Environment::EVENTS|Environment::OBJECT));
        con = env->createConnection("HR","HR","");
```

```
    }
    catch(SQLException exc){
    cout<<"In constructor "<<exc.getMessage();
    }
}

~dbc()
{
    env->terminateConnection(con);
    Environment::terminateEnvironment(env);
}


void register_notif_callback()
{
    OCISvcCtx *svchp;
    OCIError *errhp;
    OCIStmt *stmthp;
    OCIEnv *envhp;
    OCISubscription *subscrhp;
        ub4   name_space  =  OCI_SUBSCR_NAMESPACE_
DBCHANGE;
    boolean rowids_needed = TRUE;

    //OCCI
    envhp = env->getOCIEnvironment();

    checkerr(errhp,OCIHandleAlloc( (dvoid *) envhp, (dvoid
**) &errhp, OCI_HTYPE_ERROR,
            (size_t) 0, (dvoid **) 0));

    checkerr(errhp,OCIHandleAlloc ((dvoid *) envhp, (dvoid
**) &subscrhp, OCI_HTYPE_SUBSCRIPTION,
            (size_t) 0,(dvoid **) 0));
    printf("\nSubscription Handle Allocated\n");
```

```
    checkerr(errhp,OCIAttrSet (subscrhp,  OCI_HTYPE_
SUBSCRIPTION,  (dvoid *) &name_space,
                sizeof(ub4),OCI_ATTR_SUBSCR_
NAMESPACE, errhp));

/* Associate a notification callback */
    checkerr(errhp,OCIAttrSet (subscrhp,  OCI_HTYPE_
SUBSCRIPTION,(void *)notification_callback,
        0,OCI_ATTR_SUBSCR_CALLBACK, errhp));

/* Allow extraction of rowid information */
    checkerr(errhp,OCIAttrSet (subscrhp,  OCI_HTYPE_
SUBSCRIPTION,
        (dvoid *)&rowids_needed, sizeof(ub4),OCI_ATTR_
CHNF_ROWIDS,errhp));

//OCCI
svchp = con->getOCIServiceContext();

            checkerr(errhp,OCISubscriptionRegister(svchp,
&subscrhp, 1, errhp, OCI_DEFAULT));

//OCCI
stmt=con->createStatement("SELECT MANAGER_ID from
EMPLOYEES where EMPLOYEE_ID=206");
stmthp=stmt->getOCIStatement();

    checkerr(errhp,OCIAttrSet (stmthp, OCI_HTYPE_STMT,
subscrhp, 0,
            OCI_ATTR_CHNF_REGHANDLE, errhp));

stmt->execute();
printf("Registered Query. Waiting for Notifications ...\n\
n");
```

```
  while (notifications_processed != 1);

  checkerr(errhp, OCISubscriptionUnRegister(svchp,subscr
hp, errhp, OCI_DEFAULT));

  /* Free all the handles */
      OCIHandleFree((dvoid    *)subscrhp,    OCI_HTYPE_
SUBSCRIPTION);
    OCIHandleFree((dvoid  *)  errhp,  (ub4)  OCI_HTYPE_
ERROR);
 con->terminateStatement(stmt);
 }

};

int main(void)
{
 try
 {
  dbc *change_notif;
  change_notif = new dbc();
  change_notif->register_notif_callback();
 }
 catch(SQLException e)
 {
   cout<<e.getMessage()><<endl;
 }
```

☞ QUESTION 9

retrieve "Trigger_Data" within "eventHandler( )"

The received events don't seem to come with a payload.

The payload is the following:

Create type trigger_Data as Object(name as VARCHAR2(20), value as NUMBER(8))

The trigger is the following:

CREATE OR REPLACE TRIGGER PROFILE_INSERT_ TRIGGER AFTER INSERT ON PROFILE_TEST FOR EACH ROW DECLARE
queueopts DBMS_AQ.ENQUEUE_OPTIONS_T;
msgprops DBMS_AQ.MESSAGE_PROPERTIES_T;
msgid RAW(16);
my_msg Trigger_Data;

BEGIN

my_msg := Trigger_data('Profile_Test',:NEW.Value);

DBMS_AQ.ENQUEUE ('ProfileQueue',
queueopts,
msgprops,
my_msg,
msgid);

END PROFILE_INSERT_TRIGGER;

The callback function in OCCI is the following:

static unsigned int eventHandler(oracle::occi::aq:: Subscription &sub, oracle::occi::aq::NotifyResult *nr);

I created a new subscription as follows:

oracle::occi::aq::Subscription newSubscription(m_ pSubscriptionEnv);
newSubscription.setSubscriptionNamespace(oracle::occi:: aq::Subscription::NS_AQ);
newSubscription.setProtocol(oracle::occi::aq:: Subscription::PROTO_CBK);
newSubscription.setPayload(*m_pBytes);
newSubscription.setCallbackContext((void *)this);
newSubscription.setSubscriptionName("profileQueue");
newSubscription.setPresentation(oracle::occi::aq:: Subscription::PRES_DEFAULT);
newSubscription.setNotifyCallback(&CSubscription:: eventHandler);

m_vSubscriptionList.push_back(newSubscription);

m_pConn->registerSubscriptions(m_vSubscriptionList);

The function "eventHandler()" is called successfully whenever an insertion to table "profile_Test" occurs. Unfortunately, "sub.getPayload()" returns a Byte of 0 length, and "nr->getBytes()", "nr->getAnyData()", "nr->getObject()" did not return any useful data either.

How do I retrieve "Trigger_Data" within "eventHandler()"?

✍ ANSWER

You have to de-queue the message. There was a created consumer in the 'event handler', in an attempt to de-queue the message.

```
oracle::occi::aq::Consumer hConsumer(pConn)
hConsumer.setMessageIdToDequeue(nr->getMessageId());
hConsumer.setDequeueMode(DEQ_REMOVE);
hConsumer.setQueueName("ProfileQueue");

Message *pMsg = &hConsumer.receive(OBJECT,"PROFILE_
TRIGGER_DATA", "SYSTEM");

if(pMsg)
{
PROFILE_TRIGGER_DATA *pObj = (PROFILE_TRIGGER_
DATA *)(pMsg->getObject());
"
"
"
}
```

Unfortunately, "pMsg->getObject()" always fails, with an exception on 'ORA-32167' "no payload set on the message"

The message is enqueued whenever an 'INSERT' is carried out as shown below:

```
CREATE OR REPLACE TRIGGER PROFILE_INSERT_
TRIGGER AFTER INSERT ON PROFILE_TEST FOR EACH
ROW DECLARE
queueopts DBMS_AQ.ENQUEUE_OPTIONS_T;
msgprops DBMS_AQ.MESSAGE_PROPERTIES_T;
msgid RAW(16);
my_msg profile_Trigger_Data;
```

```
BEGIN

my_msg := profile_Trigger_data('Profile_Test',:NEW.Value);

DBMS_AQ.ENQUEUE ('ProfileQueue',
queueopts,
msgprops,
my_msg,
msgid);

END PROFILE_INSERT_TRIGGER;
```

☞ QUESTION 10

resolving TNS problem

I tried to write a program that makes a connection to 'Oracle 9.0 Database Server', but I got a TMS 'resolving error'.

I got a following error message:

Exception thrown
Error number: 12514
   ORA-12514: TNS: listener does not currently know of service requested in
   connect descriptor

I connected to the Oracle server using a 'Visual client', and I had to set a SID and a host name. Now in my program, I use an OCCI to connect to Oracle but I don't know how to set SID.

Can I specify a SID, or I don't need it in my C/C++ program?

How can I solve this problem?

✍ ANSWER

"$ORACLE_SID" or "TWO_TASK" might have been set by default. You can try connecting without passing the "connectString" in "createConnection".

```
Connection *con;
con = env->createConnection("scott","tiger","");
```

Oracle net problems are usually solved quickly. You can also try to use a 'sqlplus client installation' on the computer you are connecting from if you have it. The errors you get indicate that you have reached a server with a listener, but you have not supplied a 'service-name' that the listener knows. If you can connect to the database using sqlplus, try the sqlplus command "show parameter service", and it will show the you the 'database service name', which may not be the same as the sid (in single instance databases, normally sid+domain).

Make sure that you use the correct 'tnsnames' file if you are connecting using 'tnsnames' and not supplying the string directly.

☞ QUESTION 11

Setting TNS

How can I set TNS?

I read some Oracle tutorials but there was no description for that.

Where can I find sources for this?

✍ ANSWER

Here is a connect descriptor entry in a "tnsnames.ora file".

The entire descriptor is mapped to a simple name called "ORCL".

```
ORCL =
(DESCRIPTION =
(ADDRESS = (PROTOCOL = TCP)(HOST = my-db-server.
com)(PORT = 1521))
(CONNECT_DATA =
(SERVER = DEDICATED)
(SERVICE_NAME = orcl)
)
)
```

This is how I connect to 'scott schema':
$>sqlplus scott/tiger@orcl

SQL*Plus: Release 10.1.0.2.0 - Production on Wed Mar 29 14:24:00 2006

Connected to:
Oracle Database 10g Enterprise Edition Release 10.1.0.2.0 - Production
With the Partitioning, OLAP and Data Mining options

SQL>

I can even connect without specifying 'orcl' since it's already set in "ORACLE_SID":

$>echo $ORACLE_SID
orcl

$>sqlplus scott/tiger

SQL*Plus: Release 10.1.0.2.0 - Production on Wed Mar 29 14:24:00 2006

Connected to:
Oracle Database 10g Enterprise Edition Release 10.1.0.2.0 - Production
with the Partitioning, OLAP and Data Mining options

SQL>

If I try to do this:

$>sqlplus scott/tiger@wrongdescriptor

SQL*Plus: Release 10.1.0.2.0 - Production on Wed Mar 29 14:30:53 2006

ERROR:
ORA-12154: TNS:could not resolve the connect identifier specified

Enter user-name:
ERROR:
ORA-01017: invalid username/password; logon denied

This happened because 'wrong descriptor' is not there in "tnsnames.ora".

Back to the error "12154", means you are asking connection to a service which the listener is not aware of. Try the following:

$>lsnrctl services

LSNRCTL for 32-bit Windows: Version 10.1.0.2.0 - Production on 29-MAR-2006 14:44:23

Connecting to (DESCRIPTION=(ADDRESS=(PROTOCOL=I PC)(KEY=EXTPROC)))
Services Summary...

Service "orcl" has 1 instance:

Instance "orcl", status UNKNOWN, has 1 handler(s) for this service...
Handler(s):
"DEDICATED" established:420808 refused:2

LOCAL SERVER:
The command is completed successfully.

If you carefully see the "tnsnames.ora" I pasted in the beginning, the "SERVICE_NAME" parameter matched precisely to what the listener is aware of.

The "tnsnames.ora" is present in "ORACLE_HOME\network\ admin" directory. Just check if the service name you are using while connecting matches a 'service_name' entry in "tnsnames.ora".

If that is fine, try restarting the instance and the listener.

Another suggestion is to check that you don't have several 'oracle_homes' installed. Each will normally come with its own 'sqlnet-configuration'.

Don't worry about restarting the database or listener. It is just one of those things that you normally do if you can. But just to make sure, it is possible to connect to the database from other installations of 'sqlnet'. (This is to verify that there is a listener running on the machine, and it listens to the database).

In "$oracle_home/network/admin", there are 2 files of interest: "sqlnet.ora" and "tnsnames.ora".

The first contains the way to connect, and the second contains the connections. You can try to post the following:
  * the content of "sqlnet.ora";
  * the relevant portion of "tnsnames.ora";
  * and the 'sqlplus connect string' you use;

☞ QUESTION 12

query of Oracle 9.2.0.7 database

I need to do a simple query of 'Oracle 9.2.0.7 database' from either 'C' or 'C++' code on Solaris 10. I have very limited experience with either Oracle or Solaris, but have an extensive experience with 'C/C++'. I first tried to build Oracle sample program 'cdemo'. I seem to succeed to compile "cdemo81. c" and "occidml.cpp" but I can't link. I am getting a bunch of unresolved external errors with the demo 'make file demo. mk'. We have 'G++' compiler version 2.95.3 '20010315'.

How can I compile and link either a demo or a very simple application that queries Oracle database?

✍ ANSWER

You can check an OCCI basic program here:
http://www.oracle.com/technology/tech/oci/occi/occibasic. html

You can download 9.2.0 samples here:
http://www.oracle.com/technology/sample_code/tech/occi/ index.html

The "occidml.cpp" is a basic demo.

You can take a look at the Oracle supplied make file:

$ORACLE_HOME/rdbms/demo/demo_rdbms.mk.

To build an OCCI program, you can use this make file:

```
$ make -f $ORACLE_HOME/rdbms/demo/demo_rdbms.mk
buildocci
  EXE=occidml OBJS=occidml.o
```

.

☞ QUESTION 13

Downloaded "instantclient_10_2" Basic Client

I just download 'instantclient_10_2' Basic for Solaris, it unzipped to an 'instantclient_10_2' directory with following files:

classes12.jar
libclntsh.so.10.1
libnnz10.so
libocci.so.10.1
libociei.so
libocijdbc10.so
ojdbc14.jar

I have a VERY basic c++ program:

```
#include <stdio.h>
#include <occi.h>

int main()
{
return 0;
}
```

I'm using 'Sun C++ 5.8 2005/10/13' compiler on Solaris 9.

I got the following error while compiling:

   CC test.cpp -Linstantclient_10_2 -locci
   "test.cpp", line 2: Error: Could not open include file<occi.

h>.
  1 Error(s) detected.

What am I missing here?

✍ ANSWER

You can do the following:

1) Download the SDK and unzipped to the same 'instantclient_
   10_2' directory.
2) Created symbolic links in 'instantclient_10_2' directory
   for:
        In -s libocci.so.10.1 libocci.so
        In -s libclntsh.so.10.1 libclntsh.so
3) You can compile using the following:
   CC -Linstantclient_10_2 -Iinstantclient_10_2/sdk/include
   test.cpp -locci –lclntsh

☞ QUESTION 14

Problem with access to Environment

I use 'Gentoo Linux'. My problem is I can't access the 'Environment'. I tried some examples from the site, but without any positive result.

I have to write a code based on OCCI library. I will use ODBC if I can't solve the problem.

I get the following error message:

/tmp/ccf0eMaZ.o: In function `main':
a.cpp:(.text+0x208): undefined reference to `oracle::occi::Environment::createEnvironment(oracle::occi::Environment::Mode, void*, void* (*)(void*, unsigned), void* (*)(void*, void*, unsigned), void (*)(void*, void*))'
collect2: ld returned 1 exit status

I tried many examples with the same result.

Is there a solution for this?

✍ ANSWER

Check the 'gcc' version in your Linux distribution. On RedHat Linux AS 3.0, OCCI supports gcc 3.2.3 for 10.1 & 10.2.

☞ QUESTION 15

To pass array of objects to a procedure using OCCI

I have a procedure that is taken as an input in an array of objects.

Below is the code snippet:

```
create type full_name as object (first_name varchar2(20),
last_name
varchar2(20));

CREATE OR REPLACE package complex type as type enam
is table of full_name index by binary_integer;
PROCEDURE insert_Complex(e enam);
end complextype;
/
CREATE OR REPLACE package body complextype as
PROCEDURE insert_Complex(e enam)
AS
BEGIN
for i in e.first..e.last loop
INSERT INTO EMP_NAME VALUES (e(i));
end loop;
END insert_Complex;
end complextype;
```

Using OCCI, how can I bind the parameter with this? Using OTT, I created the class representation of the above object type i.e. "class full_name".

```
stmt=con->createStatement("BEGIN     complextype.insert_
Complex(:1); END;");
full_name *name1 = new full_name;
name1->setFirst_name("nishant");
name1->setLast_name("shekhar");
vect.push_back(name1);
stmt->registerOutParam(1,OCCIVECTOR,0,"FULL_
NAME");
setVector(stmt,1,vect,"FULL_NAME");
```

The above code throws an error at 'setvector' method:

"ORA-22318 input type is not an array type"

How can I resolve this problem?

✍ ANSWER

The type 'enam' is not an Oracle collection type, but a 'PL/SQL' table type. You need to create a VARRAY (or Nested table) collection type:

create type 'enam' as varray(100) of full_name;

Remove the "registerOutParam" since 'e' is an 'IN' parameter. Change the 'setVector' to:

setVector(stmt, 1, vect, "ENAM");

You can put multiple "'full_name" objects in a "vector<full_name *>", and pass it to the server with 'setVector()'.

Try passing "ENAM" (in uppercase) to setVector.

☞ QUESTION 16

OTT command line

Environment variables: "oracle_home=c:\oracle".

Command line:
    ott userid=scott/tiger intype=demoin.typ
    outtype=demoout.typ code=cpp
    hfile=demo.h cppfile=demo.cpp
    mapfile=RegisterMappings.cpp

Error message:
    Exception in thread "main" java.lang.
    NoClassDefFoundError:
    oracle/ott/c/CMain

Where should I place all the classes (not only the 'CMain. class') of oracle package?

What else should I have to configure?

✍ ANSWER

Install XE client. Set "ORACLE_HOME" to the client installation path.

*************************ott.bat*************************

@echo off
Rem OTT script for Oracle XE .
Rem Before running this script

```
Rem set jdk1.4.2/bin to PATH
Rem If ORACLE_HOME is not set, set the
Rem CLASSPATH to the directories containing
Rem ojdbc14.jar,orai18n.jar and ottclasses.zip
Rem

if defined ORACLE_HOME set CLASSPATH=%ORACLE_
HOME%\jdbc\lib\ojdbc14.jar;%ORACLE_HOME%\jlib\
orai18n.jar;%ORACLE_HOME%\precomp\lib\ottclasses.
zip;%CLASSPATH%

set NLSLANG=
if defined NLS_LANG set NLSLANG=NLS_LANG

if defined ORACLE_HOME (
java          oracle.ott.c.CMain          nlslang=%NLSLANG%
orahome=%ORACLE_HOME% %*
) else (
java oracle.ott.c.CMain nlslang=%NLSLANG% %*
)
```

☞ QUESTION 17

Retrieve data from "IN OUT VARCHAR2" variable of PL/SQL

I'm using OCCI: OCCI10gR2.

Here is a sample PL/SQL code:

```
SQL> CREATE PROCEDURE test4_proc( str IN OUT
VARCHAR2 ) IS
2 BEGIN
3 str := str || ':' || str;
4 END;
/
```

And here is a 'C++' sample code using OCCI:

```
std::string sql4 = "BEGIN test4_proc(:1); END;";
std::string result;
Statement* stmt4 = conn->createStatement(sql4);
stmt4->setString(1, "Hello");
stmt4->registerOutParam(1, OCCISTRING, 12);
stmt4->executeUpdate();
result = stmt4->getString(1);
std::cout << "<" << result << ">" << std::endl;
```

Executing this sample code, disappointingly the output is "<:>". I expected that the output would be "<Hello:Hello>".

Am I correct in my assumption?

✍ ANSWER

For an 'IN OUT parameter', you should not call "registerOutParam". Just pass the input value using 'setXXX' methods, and then read using 'getXXX'. If the output value length is greater for a 'VARCHAR2 IN OUT parameter', then the input value length should be to call "setMaxParamSize()" before calling 'setString'.

☞ QUESTION 18

OCI-22303: type not found

I created a new object type using 'SQL Plus' using the following command:

```
create type profile_Trigger_Data as object(Name
VARCHAR2(30), PRIndex
NUMBER(8));
```

I know this object is successfully created as "DESC profile_Trigger_Data". It also shows all information about the attributes.

This object and the message are enqueued whenever an 'INSERT' is carried out on a table. In my OCCI code, I tried to dequeue the message with the following code:

```
oracle::occi::aq::Consumer hConsumer(Conn);
hConsumer.setDequeueMode(oracle::occi::aq::Consumer::
DEQ_REMOVE);
hConsumer.setQueueName("ProfileQueue");

oracle::occi::aq::Message    *pMsg    =    &hConsumer.
receive(oracle::occi::aq::Message::OBJECT,"Profile_Trigger_
Data", "system");
```

Unfortunately, a 'SQLException' always occur with the following message:

OCI-22303: type "system"."profile_trigger_data" not found

Is there a solution to this problem?

✍ ANSWER

You can try passing the 'typename' and schema name in the uppercase.

You can use the following:

> oracle::occi::aq::Message   *pMsg   =   >&hConsumer. receive(oracle::occi::aq::Message::OBJECT,"Profile_Trigger_ Data", >"system");

☞ QUESTION 19

Unique constraint violation while updating a 'NON PK' column

I found a strange error. I tried to bulk fetch a cursor in some table arrays, with limit of 1000. Then, using a forall and a save exceptions at the end, I updated a table with the values inside one of the table arrays. The column I updated was not part of a PK.

I catched the error message "ORA-24381" by using 'PRAGMA' "exception_init(dml_errors, -24381)", and then later on the following:

WHEN dml_errors THEN
errors := SQL%BULK_EXCEPTIONS.COUNT;
FOR i IN 1..sql%BULK_EXCEPTIONS.count LOOP
lr_logging.parameters:= 'index = ' || sql%BULK_
EXCEPTIONS(i).error_index || 'error = ' ||Sqlerrm(-
sql%BULK_EXCEPTIONS(i).error_code) ;
END LOOP;

I inserted these errors in another table. I got 956 errors.
The first one is:
  index = 3error = ORA-00001: unique constraint (.) violated
and the last one is:
  index = 1000error = ORA-00001: unique constraint (.) violated

How did this happen since I don't update in a 'PKcolumn'?

The full code is the following:

```
PROCEDURE Update_corr_values( as_checkdate_from IN
VARCHAR2,
as_checkdate_until IN VARCHAR2,
as_market IN VARCHAR2
)
IS
LS_MODULE_NAME    CONSTANT    VARCHAR2(30)    :=
'update_values';
lr_logging recon_logging.logrec;

CURSOR lc_update IS
SELECT           /*+ORDERED*/c.rowid,c.ralve_record_id,d.
value,c.timestamp,f.value
FROM rcx_allocated_values a,
rcx_allocated_values b,
meter_histories e,
rcx_allocated_lp_value c,
rcx_allocated_lp_value d,
counter_values f
WHERE a.slp_type NOT IN ('S89', 'S88', 'S10', 'S30') --AELP
AND b.slp_type IN ('S89', 'S88') --residu
AND     a.valid_from     >=     to_date(as_checkdate_
from,'DDMMYYYY HH24:MI')
AND a.valid_to <= to_date(as_checkdate_until,'DDMMYYYY
HH24:MI')
AND a.market = as_market
AND a.market = b.market
AND a.ean_sup = b.ean_sup
AND a.ean_br = b.ean_br
AND a.ean_gos = b.ean_gos
AND a.ean_dgo = b.ean_dgo
AND a.direction = b.direction
AND a.valid_from = b.valid_from
```

```
AND a.valid_to = b.valid_to
AND c.ralve_record_id = a.record_id
AND d.ralve_record_id = b.record_id
AND c.TIMESTAMP = d.TIMESTAMP
AND e.ASSET_ID = 'KCF.SLP.' || a.SLP_TYPE
--AND    f.timestamp    between    to_date(gs_checkdate_
from,'ddmmyyyy')         and         to_Date(as_checkdate_
until,'ddmmyyyy')
AND e.SEQ = f.MHY_SEQ
AND f.TIMESTAMP =c.timestamp - 1/24
ORDER BY c.rowid;

TYPE t_value IS TABLE OF RCX_ALLOCATED_LP_VALUE.
VALUE%TYPE;
TYPE    t_kcf    IS    TABLE    OF    COUNTER_VALUES.
VALUE%TYPE;
TYPE t_timestamp IS TABLE OF RCX_ALLOCATED_LP_
VALUE.TIMESTAMP%TYPE;
TYPE t_ralverecord_id IS TABLE OF RCX_ALLOCATED_
LP_VALUE.RALVE_RECORD_ID%TYPE;
TYPE t_row IS TABLE OF UROWID;
ln_row t_row :=t_row();
lt_value t_value := t_Value();
lt_kcf t_kcf := t_kcf();
lt_timestamp t_timestamp := t_timestamp();
lt_ralve t_ralverecord_id := t_ralverecord_id();
v_bulk NUMBER := 1000;
val number;
kcf number;
ralve number;
times date;
dml_errors EXCEPTION;
errors NUMBER;
PRAGMA exception_init(dml_errors, -24381);
BEGIN
```

--setting arguments for the logging record
lr_logging.module := LS_MODULE_NAME;
lr_logging.context := 'INFLOW_ALL_VALUES_PARTS';
lr_logging.logged_by := USER;
lr_logging.parameters := 'Date time started: ' || TO_
CHAR(sysdate,'DD/MM/YYYY HH24:MI');
-- log debugs
recon_logging.set_logging_env (TRUE, TRUE);
recon_logging.log_event(lr_logging,'D');
OPEN lc_update;
LOOP
FETCH lc_update BULK COLLECT INTO ln_row,lt_ralve,lt_
value,lt_timestamp,lt_kcf LIMIT v_bulk;
FORALL i IN NVL(lt_value.first,1)..NVL(lt_value.last,0) SAVE
EXCEPTIONS
UPDATE RCX_ALLOCATED_LP_VALUE
SET VALUE = VALUE * lt_value(i) * lt_kcf(i)
WHERE rowid =ln_row(i);
COMMIT;
lt_value.delete;
lt_timestamp.delete;
lt_ralve.delete;
lt_kcf.delete;
ln_row.delete;
EXIT WHEN lc_update%NOTFOUND;
END LOOP;
CLOSE lc_update;
recon_logging.log_event(lr_logging,'D');
lr_logging.parameters := 'Date time ended: ' || TO_
CHAR(sysdate,'DD/MM/YYYY HH24:MI');
recon_logging.log_event(lr_logging,'D');
--to be sure
COMMIT;

EXCEPTION

```
WHEN dml_errors THEN
recon_logging.set_logging_env(TRUE,TRUE);
lr_logging.module := 'updatevalues';
lr_logging.context := 'exception';
lr_logging.logged_by := USER;
lr_logging.parameters := 'in dml_errors';

recon_logging.log_event(lr_logging);
errors := SQL%BULK_EXCEPTIONS.COUNT;
lr_logging.parameters:=errors;
recon_logging.log_event(lr_logging);
lr_logging.parameters :=('Number of errors is ' || errors);
--DBMS_OUTPUT.PUT_LINE('Number of errors is ' ||
errors);
FOR i IN 1..sql%BULK_EXCEPTIONS.count LOOP
lr_logging.parameters:=  'index   =  '  ||  sql%BULK_
EXCEPTIONS(i).error_index  ||  'error  =  '  ||Sqlerrm(-
sql%BULK_EXCEPTIONS(i).error_code) ;
recon_logging.log_event(lr_logging);
END LOOP;
--recon_logging.set_logging_env(TRUE,TRUE);
--recon_logging.log_event(lr_logging);
commit;
WHEN OTHERS THEN
lr_logging.module := 'updatevalues';
lr_logging.context := 'exception';
lr_logging.logged_by := USER;
recon_logging.set_logging_env(TRUE,TRUE);
lr_logging.parameters := 'in others error=' || SQLERRM;
recon_logging.log_event(lr_logging);
commit;--to look which is truly the last (else only commit
after 1000)
--raise_application_error(-20001,'An error was encountered
- '||SQLCODE||' -ERROR- '||SQLERRM);
END Update_corr_values;
```

How do I fix this?

✍ ANSWER

Check if there is a unique constraint defined on the column.

```
SQL> CREATE TABLE test_uk (id NUMBER UNIQUE)
2 /
Table created.

SQL> INSERT INTO test_uk values(1)
2 /
1 row created.

SQL> INSERT INTO test_uk values(2)
2 /
1 row created.

SQL> INSERT INTO test_uk values(1)
2 /
INSERT INTO test_uk values(1)
*
ERROR at line 1:
ORA-00001:  unique  constraint  (SCOTT.SYS_C003295)
violated

SQL> SELECT table_name,constraint_type,constraint_name
FROM USER_CONSTRAINTS
2 /

TABLE_NAME C CONSTRAINT_NAME
------------------------- - -------------------------
EMP C SYS_C003078
DEPT C SYS_C003079
TEST_UK U SYS_C003295
```

☞ QUESTION 20

Convert from char* to unsigned char*

I tried to compile an example from:

http://download-uk.oracle.com/docs/cd/B19306_01/
appdev.102/b14294/relational.htm#i1000940

It's in 'Visual C++', and I have problem with:

    const string userName = "SCOTT";

It happened because the string was defined as 'unsigned char*', and "SCOTT" is 'char*'. Is there any function to convert from 'type char*' to 'type unsigned char*'?

✍ ANSWER

Try to use:

    const string userName = (const unsigned char*)
"SCOTT";

☞ QUESTION 21

Creating a new connection instance with MSVC7.1

I got the following error:

"The instruction at "<address>" referenced memory at "<address>". The memory could not be "read".

I have 10.1.0 client installed.

I have "C:\oracle\product\10.1.0\Client_1\oci\lib\msvc\vc71" & "C:\oracle\product\10.1.0\Client_1\oci\lib\msvc" in my list of link directories. I have "C:\oracle\product\10.1.0\Client_1\oci\include" in my include directories. The problem is still there.

What can be the solution?

✍ ANSWER

In the process of transferring an existing application from OCI to OCCI, you need to link with:

    ORACLE_HOME\oci\lib\msvc (for OCI)
    ORACLE_HOME\oci\lib\msvc\vc71 (for OCCI)

The directory 'MSVC' has a version of "occi10.dll" that was getting in the way, regardless of the link order. You can remove (make a back up copy) this dll.

☞ Question 22

Pro*C application not working after upgrading to 10g

My 'Pro*C' client application uses dynamic SQL which didn't worked after upgrading Oracle client from 8.1.7 to 10g.

The application has been pre-compiled, compiled, and linked in a 10g client environment. After connecting to the DB, the first SQL statement fires a SQL "02104" error: "Inconsistent host cache. No cursor cache available":

```
EXEC SQL BEGIN DECLARE SECTION;
char outdesc[] = "output_descriptor";
EXEC SQL END DECLARE SECTION;

EXEC SQL WHENEVER SQLERROR DO MyFunc();
EXEC SQL WHENEVER NOTFOUND CONTINUE;
// Allocate descriptors for output variables
EXEC SQL ALLOCATE DESCRIPTOR :outdesc; <<--- Error
2104
```

Precompiler options are:

```
release_cursor=no
hold_cursor=no
def_sqlcode=yes
char_map=string
code=ansi_c
cpp_suffix=cpp
dbms=v8
mode=ANSI
```

sqlcheck=semantics
parse=full
dynamic=ANSI
type_code=ANSI
maxopencursors=50
pagelen=256
prefetch=5

The application is working fine on 8.1.7.

What should I do about this?

✍ ANSWER

Try to move the "ALLOCATE DESCRIPTOR" statement after a "PREPARE S FROM ...." statement:

```
EXEC SQL BEGIN DECLARE SECTION;
char outdesc[] = "output_descriptor";
EXEC SQL END DECLARE SECTION;

EXEC SQL WHENEVER SQLERROR DO MyFunc();
EXEC SQL WHENEVER NOTFOUND CONTINUE;

EXEC SQL PREPARE S FROM "SELECT ......."; <<--- moved
from (*)

// Allocate descriptors for output variables
EXEC SQL ALLOCATE DESCRIPTOR :outdesc; <<--- OK !
. . .
(*)
```

☞ QUESTION 23

pro*c compile problem

I tested 'pro*c', so I also installed Oracle 10g and its companion. I tried to find 'pro*c's' demo files, but unfortunately did not.

My OS is SuSE Linux 9.1 and gcc version is 3.3.3.

I also went to "$ORACLE_HOME/precomp/demo/proc" and type 'make', then the compiler stated:

FileServer:/oracle/app/product/10.1.0/Db_1/precomp/demo/proc # make
make: `/oracle/app/product/10.1.0/Db_1/lib/libclntsh.so' is up to date.

How can I compile or make the demo pro*c files?

✍ ANSWER

Try to make samples for C proc demos, and make 'cppsamples' for C++ demos. The "Makefile" explains how to build these samples.

☞ QUESTION 24

execute the *.sql when using occi and vc

I must initialize the remote database using the file of sql. For example:

The file is "ss.sql" as shown below:

```
"DECLARE
row integer := 0;
user varchar2(256);
BEGIN
user := '&1';
dbms_java.grant_policy_permission('PUBLIC', 'SYS',
'java.lang.RuntimePermission', 'loadLibrary.*', row);
dbms_java.grant_permission(user,              'SYS:java.lang.
RuntimePermission',
'loadLibrary.orawcom10', null);
dbms_java.disable_permission(row);
dbms_java.delete_permission(row);
EXCEPTION
WHEN OTHERS THEN
IF row > 0 THEN
dbms_java.disable_permission(row);
dbms_java.delete_permission(row);
END IF;
RAISE;
END;"
```

I used the occi statement:

```
Environment * env;
Connection * conn;
```

```
Statement * stmt;
env=Environment::createEnvironment(Environment::
DefaultEnvironment);
conn=env->createConnect(user_name,pwd,db_name);
string sqlstmt="BEGIN ss.sql;END";
stmt=conn->createStatement(sqlstmt);
```

It was wrong.

How can I change the sql statement?

✍ ANSWER

Instead of having the 'PL/SQL' code as an anonymous block, you can create a procedure and then execute it through OCCI.
For example:

```
create or replace procedure my_proc
is
row integer := 0;
user varchar2(256);
begin
--code here...
end;
```

Assuming that this code will be in "ss.sql". Compile this procedure in
your schema, and then form the "sqlstmt" in OCCI this way:

```
    Statement *stmt = con->createStatement("BEGIN my_
proc; END;") ;
```

DCL statements are used mainly for administration of user

privileges and access rights to Oracle. The "@ syntax" is more of a SQL Plus command to execute
scripts, and cannot be used to execute 'pl/sql' code from a programmatic interface like OCCI or OCI.

☞ QUESTION 25

SQL store_result

I'm selecting a table with 300,000 rows.

Calling "ResultSet->Next()" is getting one row at the time, and over
the internet that is very slow. On my SQL, there is a function named "mysql_store_result", which gets all the select data in one chunk into memory. Then, I can process one row at the time without making a fetch over the net each time.

How can I do that in Oracle?

✍ ANSWER

"setPrefetchRowCount" (on the statement object) will do just that.

"setPrefetchRowCount()" 'pre-fetches' the specified number of rows to the client in a single round-trip. The subsequent "rs->next()" calls are purely local.

☞ QUESTION 26

createEnvironment(Environment: THREADED_MUTEXED)

Do I have to specify my own 'thread-safe' memory management functions when I want to use "createEnvironment(THREADE D_MUTEXED)"? Or will OCCI use its own internal 'thread-safe' memory management functions if I don't specify any memory management functions when invoking "createEnvironment"?

✍ ANSWER

If you call "createEnvironment" with "THREADED_ MUTEXED" as the mode, OCCI would serialize all the 'thread-safe' objects in that environment. The application doesn't need to do it.

However, if you wish to have your own mutexing scheme, you can pass the mode as "THREADED_UNMUTEXED", and allow your application to exclusively lock OCCI calls made on objects in that environment. Take note that when the mode is "THREADED_UNMUTEXED", OCCI will assume that your application will take care of mutexing and will not acquire its own mutexes.

☞ QUESTION 27

Using ORACA in Pro*C program

I wanted to use the ORACA structure in my 'Pro*C' program for reporting the SQL statement, source file, and line number if an error is encountered. I've read that it is not enabled by default, because it impacts performance. I can't find the extent of the impact. In particular, if I don't enable any of the debugging options or the master debug flag, and only set "oraca.orastxtf = ORASTFERR", the SQL text is only copied if there's an error.

Is this a significant impact, or this is just an issue left over from the days of 8MHz processors?

✍ ANSWER

There should not be a significant impact to setting the "oraca. orastxtf = ORASTFERR". Any impact that is present will not have effect on the steady state performance, only on the error cases.

☞ QUESTION 28

ORA-22884: object modification failed

Why does the following fail with ORA-22884?

SwitchContext *context = new(sessConn, "SWITCH_ CONTEXTS_V")SwitchContext;
context->setStatus(SwitchContext::WAITING);
sessConn->commit();

...

context->setStatus(SwitchContext::PROCESSED);
context->markModified();
sessConn->commit();

Insert and update trigger defined appears to work with "Ref<SwitchContext>" instead.

How do I correct the situation?

✍ ANSWER

You cannot use direct object pointers beyond transaction boundaries, you need to use 'Refs'.

☞ Question 29

invalid LOB locator specified

"Blob: ORA-22275: invalid LOB locator specified"

I got this error message shown above if I execute the following code:

```
Statement *stmt = conn->createStatement ("INSERT INTO
electronic_media(product_id,ad_id,ad_composite,ad_
sourcetext) VALUES (:v1,:v2,:v3,:v4)");
Blob blob(conn);
blob.setEmpty();
Clob clob(conn);
clob.setEmpty();
stmt->setInt(1,6666);
stmt->setInt(2,11001);
int size = 5;
unsigned int offset=1;
unsigned char *buffer = new unsigned char[size];
memset (buffer, (char)10, size);
unsigned     int     bytesWritten=blob.write     (size,buffer,
size,offset);
delete[] buffer;
stmt->setBlob(3,blob);
stmt->setClob(4,clob);
stmt->executeUpdate();
```

Is there a solution for this?

✍ Answer

You need to insert the row in the table, returning an empty blob like this:

```
INSERT INTO table (ID, FILENAME, FILE_BLOB, ...)
    VALUES (seq_table_pk.nextval(), 'filename.txt', empty_
blob(), ...)
    RETURN FILE_BLOB INTO :lobfile;
```

And then, you can use 'lobfile' to load your blob:

```
bf := BFILENAME( p_dirlob, p_filename );

IF DBMS_LOB.FILEEXISTS( bf ) = 1 THEN

IF DBMS_LOB.ISOPEN (bf) = 1 THEN
DBMS_LOB.FILECLOSE (bf);
END IF;

IF DBMS_LOB.GETLENGTH( bf ) = 0 THEN
- Manage your error
ELSE
DBMS_LOB.OPEN( bf, DBMS_LOB.LOB_READONLY );
DBMS_LOB.LOADFROMFILE( lobfile, bf, DBMS_LOB.
GETLENGTH( bf ), 1, 1 );
DBMS_LOB.FILECLOSE(bf);
END IF;
```

END IF;

This is 'PL/SQL' in a proc. You have to declare your directory (here, 'DIRLOB') on the server where the instance of your DB is, and that you have to get 'rights' (at least 'read') on it. The variable 'bF' is a "BFILE".

☞ QUESTION 30

XML insert using OCCI

I'm looking for some sample code that uses the OCCI to insert 'xml' documents into the "10g XML DB".

I have an application running on UNIX that is subscribing to a topic, and receives small 'xml documents' (10k) upon publication. The application then simply inserts the 'xml' documents into the 10g db.

Are there any good books on "XML-OCCI" programming?

✍ ANSWER

If the 'XML' document is to be inserted in an 'exists' as a file stored on a disk, you can insert or store the 'XML' document as 'CLOB'.

OCCI demos can be downloaded from the OCCI home page on OTN:

http://www.oracle.com/technology/sample_code/tech/occi/index.html

'CLOB' samples can be found there. The 'XML' documents will be in the memory upon subscription to a 'pub/sub' server.

☞ QUESTION 31

Compiling Oracle OCCI 10g on SunOS 5.8 sun4u sparc SUNW, Sun-Fire

I'm using Sun cc compiler, OCCI from Oracle 10g, and SunOS 5.8 sun4u sparc SUNW, Sun-Fire.

Command:

```
CC -D_LARGEFILE_SOURCE -D_FILE_OFFSET_BITS='64'
-xarch=v9 –
        I/Oracle/Oracle_Client/instantclient_10_2/sdk/include
connect.cpp
```

I wrote a 'C++' program to connect to oracle. The program did not compile and it gave me the following error:

oracle::occi::__RTTI__1nGoracleEocciMSQdDLException_
OracleTableUnload.o
[Hint: static member oracle::occi::__RTTI__1nGoracleEocci
MSQdDLException_
must be defined in the program]

oracle::occi::Environment*oracle::occi::Environment::crea
teEnvironment(oracle::occi::Environment::Mode,void*,vo
id*(*)(void*,unsigned   long),void*(*)(void*,void*,unsigned
long),void(*)(void*,void*)) OracleTableUnload.o

What else do I need to do to make it work?

✍ ANSWER

You need to add the OCCI library "libocci.so" and Oracle client library "libclntsh.so" to your command line:

"L/Oracle/Oracle_Client/instantclient_10_2/sdk/lib -locci -lclntsh"

☞ QUESTION 32

Error Handling with OCCI

Is there any function available in OCCI to register user defined function with error handler, "just like RougeWave setErrorHandler"?

✍ ANSWER

OCCI uses 'C++' exceptions (OCCI class 'SQLException') mechanism for errors.

☞ QUESTION 33

OCCI support

When will OCCI support GNU GCC v3.3.2?

When will Oracle release OCCI to support GCC 3.2 or a newer version of GCC?

I plan to estimate OCCI on 'GCC 3.2.*' for Solaris and Linux, to help us make a
decision on when to deploy OCCI solution to our customers for the solution of a Java application performance issue.

Is this advisable?

✍ ANSWER

It really depends. If it is RedHat Linux 'AS3.0/4.0', OCCI 10.2 is supported with 'gcc3.2.3' only. It may be supported with gcc3.4.3 in the future.

☞ QUESTION 34

c++ compiler for OCCI development at Solaris

Which 'C++' compiler is best to use to compile OCCI codes at Solaris?

✍ ANSWER

The information can be obtained from Oracle 'Metalink Note# 43208.1'. Below is the snapshot of which 'C++' compiler should be used for OCCI version 10.2.0:

...

SOLARIS SPARC

=============

...

9.2.0 Sun Forte Workshop 6.2 111678-13, 111679-08, (64 bit)
111681-01, 111683-08, 111685-10, 111690-07,
111691-06, 111719-02.
* 10.1.0 Sun ONE Studio 8, C/C++ 5.5
* 10.2.0 Sun ONE Studio 8, C/C++ 5.5

☞ QUESTION 35

gcc compiler for occi 9i

What gcc compiler is supported for 'OCCI 9iR2 at x86' machine, with red hat linux AS 3.0?

I'm using gcc3.

✍ ANSWER

You need to use gcc 2.96 in '9iR2'. OCCI in 10g supports gcc 3.2.3 and gcc 2.96.

☞ QUESTION 36

SuSE: OCCI segfault in getString

I am using 'SuSE9.3' with gcc 3.3.5 (libstdc++.so.5.0.7) but the "ResultSet::getString" function still fails with 'segfault':

Thread [0] (Suspended: Signal 'SIGSEGV' received. Description: Segmentation fault.)
4 oracle::occi::ResultSetImpl::checkNullAndTrunc()
3 oracle::occi::ResultSetImpl::getString()
2 ResultToStringHelper::getObjectAsString() at main. cpp:148
1 main() at main.cpp:196

The code that caused this is:

..
string res = rs->getResultSet()->getString(index);
..

The field column I tried to read has a type "OCCI_TYPECODE_ VARCHAR".

For any case, the ldd output for execution is the following:

linux-gate.so.1 => (0xffffe000)
libclntsh.so.10.1 => /usr/lib/libclntsh.so.10.1 (0x40038000)
libnnz10.so => /usr/lib/libnnz10.so (0x40bd5000)
libocci.so.10.1 => /usr/lib/libocci.so.10.1 (0x40d68000)
libociei.so => /usr/lib/libociei.so (0x40e22000)
libocijdbc10.so => /usr/lib/libocijdbc10.so (0x44b69000)
libstdc++.so.5 => /usr/lib/libstdc++.so.5 (0x44b7e000)
libm.so.6 => /lib/tls/libm.so.6 (0x44c3d000)
libgcc_s.so.1 => /lib/libgcc_s.so.1 (0x44c60000)

libc.so.6 => /lib/tls/libc.so.6 (0x44c68000)
libdl.so.2 => /lib/libdl.so.2 (0x44d81000)
libpthread.so.0 => /lib/tls/libpthread.so.0 (0x44d85000)
libnsl.so.1 => /lib/libnsl.so.1 (0x44d97000)
/lib/ld-linux.so.2 (0x40000000)

What do I do next?

✍ ANSWER

The indexing in "get****" should begin from 1, not from zero. Trying to call "getString(0)" you will get the 'segfault' above. The conclusion from this message for oracle is to consider the idea of throwing the 'SQLException', or do any debug output on invalid input data. That would save users time on error correction.

☞ QUESTION 37

Missing library files while compiling

I'm using the following: Operating System: Sun Solaris 10; DB Client Access: Oracle Instant Client 10.2.0.1; Installed path is "/apps/instantclient/instantclient_10_2"; C++ Compiler: Sun C++ Compiler 5.6.

The following are set to the above installed path: Environment variables, "LD_LIBRARY_PATH", 'PATH' and 'SQLPATH'.

My compilation settings are the following:

CC -c -o OraOperator.o -c -g -I/apps/instantclient/instantclient_10_2/sdk/include OraOperator.cpp

CC -c -o TestOCCI.o -c -g -I/apps/instantclient/instantclient_10_2/sdk/include TestOCCI.cpp

CC -g -o TestOCCI -L/apps/instantclient/instantclient_10_2 OraOperator.o TestOCCI.o -locci -lclntsh

But I got the following errors:

ld: fatal: library -locci: not found
ld: fatal: library -lclntsh: not found
ld: fatal: File processing errors. No output written to TestOCCI

Can you give me any idea on how to solve this?

✍ ANSWER

If you want to compile OCCI 64-bit with 'C/C++ 5.5' and above, under Sun Solaris SPARC-64, all you need to do is to specify the flag "-xarch=v9" at your compilation scripts.

For example:

CC -c -o TestOCCI.o -c -g -xarch=v9 -I/apps/instantclient/
instantclient_10_2/sdk/include TestOCCI.cpp

CC -c -o OraOperator.o -c -g -xarch=v9 -I/apps/instantclient/
instantclient_10_2/sdk/include OraOperator.cpp

CC -g -o TestOCCI -xarch=v9 -L/apps/instantclient/instantclient_
10_2 TestOCCI.o OraOperator.o -locci –lclntsh

☞ QUESTION 38

Connection Pool and Statement reuse

I have a (multithreaded) middle tier component that uses a connection pool and does the entire database access. Since we have many SQL statements that are reused over and over, I wanted to reuse these statements (with bind variables) and bypass the 'parse' phase.

My first plan was to simply create a statement object and set its SQL property, and then reuses it every time. But the problem is that the statement is created by the connection object, and since I'm using a connection pool and doesn't keep a pointer to the connections, I think this won't work. Another obvious problem is the use of the same statement object by different threads, which I guess is not supported.

Which is the best way to optimize my database access in this scenario? One constraint is that we're still using Oracle 9i, so it's not possible to use the (client side) 'Statement caching' feature (I think it's only available in Oracle 10).

Is there a way to just keep some information like the 'parsed SQL statement' and just bind the variables, and then reuse it over and over again?

✍ ANSWER

Note that 'OCCI/OCI Statement caching feature' caches 'SQL parse' information and execution plans. Subsequent re-executes of a cached statement is faster. Just re-using a Statement handle on the client will only save allocation costs.

☞ QUESTION 39

Statement reuse

A transactional process must perform for each request received, the same 'SQL Statement' through passing different values to the bind variables.

I tried to do the following:
1) Create the statement once, reusing the same handle and bringing the needed variables at each request.
2) Create the statement, cache it, and then for each request do a "createStatement ( )" to get it from the cache, bind the needed variables through "statementhandle->setxxx" (bindposition) and a "terminateStatement" (handle, tagvalue) to release it back to the cache.

Both behavior resulted to the following:
- low parse count on the server (actually, the statement was parsed once);
- continuous memory increase on the client side (far more than the OCCI cache).

On the other hand, disabling the statement caching, and creating or binding or terminating the statement for each request results to:
- high parse count on the server (statement parsed every time);
- stable memory usage on the client side.

Depending on the statement, any opened "ResultSet" is closed after fetching data, any object fetched with "getObject" is expicitly deleted, and any reference fetched with "getRef" is reset to null with "Ref.setNull()" etc.

I got the same behavior with 'SELECT' statement (executeQuery), calls to PL/SQL procedure (execute) either with 'IN' or 'OUT' parameters only, and mixed 'IN' and 'IN/OUT'.

How can I release any resource associated to the 'Statement' (bind variables are remembered) without the need to terminate (and reparse) the statement itself?

I'm using Oracle Server 10.1.0.3 and 9.2.0.4; Oracle Client 10.1.0.2 plus; One-Off patches p3671655_10102_TRU64, p3748199_10102_TRU64, p4055603_10102_TRU64, p4290149_10102_TRU64.

I'm on HP Tru64 5.1b Patch kit 5. What else can I use?

✍ ANSWER

For the continuous memory increase when re-binding and re-executing the same 'Statement', you can use "bug #3853332". Check if there is a patch available for this bug on HP Tru64.

☞ QUESTION 40

OCCI program compilation

The following is a program I wrote in OCCI:

Database : Oracle 10g (10.2)
OS: UNIX (AIX 5.3)
COMPILER> xlc++

This is my '.cpp' file for my program:

```
#include <iostream.h>
#include <stdio.h>
#include <occi.h>

using namespace std;
using namespace oracle::occi;

string UserName = "SCOTT";
string Password = "TIGER";
string ConnectionString = "SDPA";

int main()
{
Environment* env;
Connection* conn;
try
{
env = Environment::createEnvironment (Environment::
DEFAULT);
conn = env->createConnection (UserName, Password,
ConnectionString);
}
```

```
catch (SQLException ex)
{
cout << "Error occured" << endl;
}
Statement* stmt = conn->createStatement ();
cout << "Connected to the database " << endl;

conn->terminateStatement (stmt);
env->terminateConnection (conn);
Environment::terminateEnvironment (env);
return 0;
}
```

This is my "makefile first_db.mk":
(I included preceeding 'TABS' before commands in dependencies that will not appear in the post.)

```
#makefile for db_first.cpp
INCLUDES=-I$(ORACLE_HOME)/rdbms/demo          -I$(ORACLE_HOME)/rdbms/public   -I$(ORACLE_HOME)/plsql/public -I$(ORACLE_HOME)/network/public
CFLAGS= -O -xarch=v9

#Dynamic libraries to use: to use libocci.so, write -locci. -lclntsh is also necessary
LDLIB= -locci -lclntsh

#Directories where to find *.so
LDIRS= -L$(ORACLE_HOME)/lib
SOURCES=first_db.cpp
OBJECTS=first_db.o

#Your exe
TARGET=first_db
```

#The compiler to use
COMPILER=xlc++

#What to do
all: first_db clean
#clean removes *.o after the exe has been generated, you
can change that
clean: rm *.o

#Generate the .o
first_db.o: first_db.cpp
$(COMPILER) $(INCLUDES) -c first_db.cpp -o first_db.o

#Generate the exe
first_db: first_db.o
$(COMPILER)   first_db.o $(LDIRS) $(LDLIB)   -o
$(TARGET)

After this, when I issued the command:

make -f first_db.mk build EXE=first_db OBJS=first_db.o

I got the following error:

make: 1254-002 Cannot find a rule to create target build
from dependencies.
Stop.
How can I correct the problem? What things am I missing?

✍ ANSWER

You can take look at the Oracle supplied makefile:

$ORACLE_HOME/rdbms/demo/demo_rdbms.mk.

To build an OCCI program, you can use this makefile:

```
$ make -f $ORACLE_HOME/rdbms/demo/demo_rdbms.
mk buildocci
    EXE=first OBJS=first.o
```

☞ QUESTION 41

binary compatibility between a VS2005(VC8) compiled C++ application and a VS2003(VC71) compiled C++ library

I compiled a simple OCCI application that connects to a database & fetches some rows with VC8, and linked with the VC7.1 "oraocci10.lib/dll" that comes with Oracle 10.2 and it worked.

Do you have any reference information from Microsoft regarding binary compatibility between a "VS2005(VC8) compiled C++ application" and a "VS2003(VC71) compiled C++ library"?

✍ ANSWER

Unless it changes with 10.2, the problem with 10.1.x and VS 2005 is related with the C Runtime (MSVCR71.DLL and MSVCR71D.DLL).

"ORAOCCI10.DLL" uses "MSVCR71.DLL", and "ORAOCCI10D.DLL" uses "MSVCR71D.DLL". But "VS 2005 C++" applications need to use "MSVCR80 / 80D".

Then if you install ".NET Framework V2.0", then you have only "MSVCR80 / 80D". If you also have ".NET Framework V1.1", and "MSVCR71 / 71D", the final execution will try to run with two versions of the C Runtime.

Maybe you have linked "oraocci10.dll" (using msvcr71.dll), but compiled with 'DEBUG' (therefore, everything else uses "msvcr80D.dll"). In this case, you have a 'DEBUG' execution using a 'NON DEBUG' set of DLL's. Maybe it works, but I wouldn't bet on a 'SQLException' raised with 'NON DEBUG' runtime and catch with 'DEBUG' runtime.

☞ QUESTION 42

create temporary CLOB function

In OCI, there is a function support 'create' and a free temporary 'CLOB'.

Is there any function in OCCI that does the same thing? I can't find any function in "occi api doc".

✍ ANSWER

The only way I found is to call the "DBMS_LOB" package as:

```
#define   STMT_CREATE_CLOB   "BEGIN   DBMS_LOB.
CREATETEMPORARY (:1, TRUE); END;"
oracle::occi::Clob workClob;

cmdCreateCLOB  =  session->createStatement ( STMT_
CREATE_CLOB );
cmdCreateCLOB->registerOutParam   (1,   oracle::occi::
OCCICLOB);
cmdCreateCLOB->execute ();
workCLOB = cmdCreateCLOB->getClob (1);
```

Then you can read/write from the 'Clob LOCATOR', and use it as an "IN", "OUT", "IN OUT" parameter for PL/SQL calls.

☞ QUESTION 43

resultset::getstring()

```
#include<iostream>
#include<string>
using namespace std;
#ifndef occi_ORACLE
#define WIN32COMMON
#include "occi.h"
#pragma     comment(lib,"D:\\oracle\\product\\10.1.0\\Db_1\\
oci\\lib\\msvc\\vc6\\oraocci10.lib")
using namespace oracle::occi;
#endif

int main()
{

Environment *env=Environment::createEnvironment(Envir
onment::OBJECT);
Connection  *conn=env->createConnection("scott","tiger","
orcl");
string sqlStmt="select * from emp";
Statement *stmt=conn->createStatement(sqlStmt);
ResultSet *rset=stmt->executeQuery();
try
{
while(rset->next())
{
//when I use cout<<rset->getInt1);it is right

//when it is the statement,it is wrong.
cout<<"  "<<rset->getString(2);
```

```
}
}catch(SQLException ex)
{
cout<<"chucuole"<<endl;
}
stmt->closeResultSet(rset);
conn->terminateStatement(stmt);
env->terminateConnection(conn);
Environment::terminateEnvironment(env);
}
```

I used the 'msvc' and oracle 10 when I compiled this application. There was no error, but when I run it, it got only one result which is 'SMITH', and a pop-up window "debug assertion failed": "file:dbgheap.c,line:1001".

When I use "cout<<rest->getInt(1)", it is right. My setting is: win32debug, run time library debug multithreaded DLL, preprocessor definitions have "_MT,_DLL", object/library modules include:kernel32.lib user32.lib gdi32. lib winspool.lib comdlg32.lib advapi32.lib shell32.lib ole32. lib oleaut32.lib uuid.lib odbc32.lib odbccp32.lib.

How can I correct the error?

✍ ANSWER

There is an easy method to solve the "getString()" problem. You should add the 'lib' to your "application.project settings->link->category(input)->object/library modules:msvcprt. lib".

☞ QUESTION 44

OCCI setString

I started exploring 'occi.h' (oracle version 9.2.0), but encountered a problem.

```
#include <iostream>
#include <occi.h>
using namespace oracle::occi;
using namespace std;

int main()
{
// declare Environment, Connection, ResultSet, Statement
env=Environment::createEnvironment(Environment::
DEFAULT);
con=env->createConnection("myname",          "mypws",
"myConString");
stmt=con->createStatement("select * from aTable where
aFld=:1 and bFld=:2");
stmt->setInt(1, 10);
stmt->setString(2, "myValue");
rs=stmt->executeQuery();
rs->next();
// cout result, all fields empty, seems a result not found

stmt=con->createStatement("select * from aTable where
aFld=10 and bFld='myValue'");
rs=stmt->executeQuery();
rs->next();
```

// cout result, got the record and print expected result.

```
// close connection on env, rs, stmt, con
}
```

The difference between the first and second SQL statement is, one was parameterized and the other was not. If in the first SQL statement, I have "code:2" to 'myValue', and then execute "setInt()" only, it worked well. So, it is the "setString()" function that didn't work.

Is there a solution for this?

✍ ANSWER

You can change the SQL statement to "select * from aTable where aFld=:1 and trim(bFld)=:2". Or you can change "myValue" to "myValue<+ 3 space".

☞ QUESTION 45

OCI_ATTR_PASSWORD

I created an OCCI application with 'Visual C++'. I received the following error in the code when it tried to connect:

ORA-24960: the attribute OCI_ATTR_PASSWORD is greater than the maximum allowable length of 255.

My password is less than 10 characters.

How do I correct the issue?

✍ ANSWER

If you carefully look at "oraocci10.dll", you will know it builds using "VS .NET 2003". You should use "VS .NET 2003" (VC71) to build your OCCI application. You could also use 'VC6' with '10.1 Instant Client'.

☞ QUESTION 46

compilation under Solaris

I'm trying to compile the following test code:

```
#include <occi.h>
#include <iostream>

using namespace std;

using namespace oracle::occi;

int main(int argc, char ** argv)
{
Environment *env;
Connection * conn;
try{
env = Environment::createEnvironment();
conn = env->createConnection(user, pass, sid);

env->terminateConnection(conn);

Environment::terminateEnvironment(env);
} catch (SQLException &e) {
cout<<"Exception: %s\n", e.getNLSMessage(env).c_str();
}
return 0;
}
```

My system is Solaris 9 sparc 64-bit, and Oracle Database 10.1.0.2.

When I run this command:

CC -I/u00/oracle/product/10.1.0/db_1/rdbms/public -L/u00/oracle/product/10.1.0/db_1/lib -locci10 test.cpp

and got an error:

Undefined first referenced symbol in file
void oracle::occi::Environment::terminateEnvironment(oracle::occi::Environment*) test.o
oracle::occi::Environment*oracle::occi::Environment::createEnvironment(oracle::occi::Environment::Mode,void*,void*(*)(void*,unsigned),void*(*)(void*,void*,unsigned),void(*)(void*,void*)) test.o
oracle::occi::__RTTI__1nGoracleEocciMSQdDLException_ test.o
[Hint: static member oracle::occi::__RTTI__1nGoracleEocciMSQdDLException_ must be defined in the program]

ld: fatal: Symbol referencing errors. No output written to a.out

I tried to use:

gcc 3.4.2
Sun Forte 6.0
Sun Forte 6.2
Sun Forte 7
Sun Studio 10
All turned out the same.

If I set "LD_LIBRARY_PATH" and try to link with "*.so library", it gave me: "wrong ELF class: ELFCLASS64"

I've tried to install and use Client 10.2, but there was no effect. Under Windows, it worked perfectly.

What should I do to make this compile under Solaris?

✍ ANSWER

If you want your application to be 32 bit, you can use 'Sun Forte 6.2' and link with OCCI library under "$ORACLE_HOME/lib32".

If you want your application to be 64 bit, you can use 'Sun Forte 8' and link with libraries under "$ORACLE_HOME/lib". You should be passing the 64 bit compile flag "-xarch=v9".

☞ QUESTION 47

Configuring MSVC++ OCCI

I'm trying to connect to an Oracle10g database using "Microsoft Visual Studio .NET 2003 IDE". I am using a 'Win32 Console app'.

I used the following configuration:

C/C++, General, Additional Include Directories: $ORACL_HOME\oci\include
Linker, General, Additional Library Directories: $ORACLE_HOME\oci\lib\msvc\vc71
Linker, Input, Additional Dependencies: oraocci10.lib

I have included the code below which compiles and links. When I run it, it terminates throwing "Unhandled exception at ... ", then the debug goes to:

```
>Connection *conn = env->createConnection("SCOTT",
"TIGER");
```

What can I do to fix this problem?

```
#include "stdafx.h"
#include <occi.h>
#include <occiCommon.h>
#include <occiControl.h>
#include <occiData.h>
#include <occiObjects.h>
#include <string.h>

using namespace oracle::occi;
```

```cpp
using namespace std;

int main()
{

//const string username = "scott";
//const string password = "tiger";
//const string connString = "";
int dept;
Environment *env = Environment::createEnvironment();
try{
Connection *conn = env->createConnection("SCOTT",
"TIGER");
Statement *stmt = conn->createStatement("select deptno
from emp");
ResultSet *rs = stmt->executeQuery();
while(rs->next()== true)
{
dept = rs->getInt(1);
cout<<dept<<endl;
}
stmt->closeResultSet(rs);
env->terminateConnection(conn);
Environment::terminateEnvironment(env);
}catch(exception &str)
{
cout<<"Exeception : " << str.what() << endl;
}

return 0;

}
```

✍ Answer

Make sure that you are using the "/MD flag" of MSVC (and not "/MDd" - debug runtime libraries). If you are on 10gR1, then "ORACLE_HOME\oci\lib\msvc\vc71" should be first in the 'PATH', because the "oraocci10.dll" under "$ORACLE_HOME\bin" is for MSVC6.

☞ Question 48

Serving multiple clients using one thread

We need to create a middleware between oracle and clients, using OCI or OCCI interface.

I've read the documents and found that support for non-blocking requests to db is rather limited. I.e. I can't serve multiple clients via one thread with non blocking db queries, and async notification events on query completion (not supported).

Am I right here?

✍ Answer

OCCI does not support non-blocking mode of database access. For a middle tier, I recommend to create multiple threads to serve multiple clients. You can use OCCI "Connection pooling" or "Session pooling" to access the database. These two pooling features provide high concurrency, scalability, and optimal use of server resources. You can create other threads for non-database access.

☞ **QUESTION 49**

getString problem with RAW columns

I have a problem with 'getString' on AIX 5.3, and Oracle 9.2.0.1 when retrieving 'RAW' fields. This problem did not exist on Solaris.

When I use 'getString' to get a data from a 'RAW(16)' column in a loop, the first call works fine and the rest returns with incorrect information. In fact, all subsequent calls in that loop returned the same incorrect value.

I can use 'getBytes' and then a 'printf' "%02X" to see the data correctly, but that may take a toll on performance as I have a lot of these 'RAW' fields to deal with.

I created a table like this:

```
TESTTAB
RAWCOL RAW(16)
STRINGCOL CHAR(32)
```

I populated the rows with the same data in each column such that for a given row, a "select *" would return the same data from each field.

Then, I ran this program segment:

```
string sqlStmt = "SELECT RAWCOL, STRINGCOL FROM TESTTAB";

cout << "SQL: [" << sqlStmt << "]" << endl;
```

```
Statement *stmt;
stmt = conn->createStatement(sqlStmt);
ResultSet *rset = stmt->executeQuery ();
try
{
while (rset->next ())
{
Bytes oid = rset->getBytes(1);
string tmpStr2 = rset->getString(2);

cout << "RAWCOL AS BYTES[";
for (int i = 0; i < oid.length(); i++)
{
printf("%02X", oid.byteAt(i));
}
cout << "] STRINGCOL: [" << tmpStr2 << "]"<< endl;
}
}
```

The ouput from that is correct as shown below:

SQL: [SELECT RAWCOL, STRINGCOL FROM TESTTAB]
RAWCOL AS BYTES[C0A80165000BD0EC434D5477000B89
04]
STRINGCOL: [C0A80165000BD0EC434D5477000B8904]

RAWCOL AS BYTES[C0A80165000BD0EC434D5477000B91
58]
STRINGCOL: [C0A80165000BD0EC434D5477000B9158]

RAWCOL AS BYTES[C0A80165000BD0EC434D5477000B98
FF]
STRINGCOL: [C0A80165000BD0EC434D5477000B98FF]

Then, I run this code:

```
string sqlStmt = "SELECT RAWCOL, STRINGCOL FROM
TESTTAB";

cout << "SQL: [" << sqlStmt << "]" << endl;

Statement *stmt;
stmt = conn->createStatement(sqlStmt);
ResultSet *rset = stmt->executeQuery ();
try
{
while (rset->next ())
{
Bytes oid = rset->getBytes(1);
string tmpStr = rset->getString(1);
string tmpStr2 = rset->getString(2);

cout << "RAWCOL AS BYTES[";
for (int i = 0; i < oid.length(); i++)
{
printf("%02X", oid.byteAt(i));
}
cout << "] RAWCOL AS STRING: [" << tmpStr << "]
STRINGCOL: [" << tmpStr2 << "]"<< endl;

}
}
```

And the output is as follows:

SQL: [SELECT RAWCOL, STRINGCOL FROM TESTTAB]
RAWCOL AS BYTES [C0A80165000BD0EC434D5477000B89
04]
RAWCOL AS STRING: [C0A80165000BD0EC434D5477000B8

904]
STRINGCOL: [C0A80165000BD0EC434D5477000B8904]

RAWCOL AS BYTES [43304138303136353030304244304543]
RAWCOL AS STRING: [43304138303136353030303042443045443]
STRINGCOL: [C0A80165000BD0EC434D5477000B9158]

RAWCOL AS BYTES [43304138303136353030304244304543]
RAWCOL AS STRING: [43304138303136353030303042443045443]
STRINGCOL: [C0A80165000BD0EC434D5477000B98FF]

You can notice that the 'STRINGCOL' is always right, and doing a 'getString' on the 'RAWCOL', hosed up the data not only in the "RAWCOL AS STRING", but also when getting the column as bytes and then converting.

What other information can I provide to help diagnose this situation?

✍ ANSWER

This looks like bug "#2610331", it can be fixed in 9.2.0.4.0 and 10g. It is better to upgrade to the latest 9.2 patch or 10g patch.

☞ QUESTION 50

Cannot query array of object types

I am attempting to query the "diminfo" field of the view "MDSYS.all_sdo_geom_metadata". The field is "described" as "MDSYS.SDO_DIM_ARRAY", which is a varray of "MDSYS. SDO_DIM_ELEMENT".

I run OTT to generate the class files, but nothing is generated for the "MDSYS.SDO_DIM_ARRAY" type. A class is generated for the "SDO_DIM_ELEMENT" objects.

Anyway, I tried to query the field using both "VALUE(diminfo)" and "REF(diminfo)":

select VALUE(diminfo) from all_sdo_geom_metadata;
- or -
select REF(diminfo) from all_sdo_geom_metadata;

I got an ORA-904 "invalid identifier". When I remove the "VALUE" or "REF" from the query, the error goes away and was replaced by an 'ORA-32162' "Read/Write method not registered" further down in the code when I try to retrieve the value from the record set:

    myDimInfo = rSet->getObject(1);

Since the field type (MDSYS.SDO_DIM_ARRAY) isn't really an object type, I can see why the "Read/Write method not registered" occurs, there are no methods to register.

Can someone provide a code snippet on how to perform this query?

✍ ANSWER

OTT generates 'C++' class declarations for object types (i.e. for "SDO_DIM_ELEMENT"). A collection (varray or nested table) is represented by the "STL vector<T>" class in OCCI.

You will have to the following:
1) Call the OTT generated register mappings function after the 'Environment' is created, and before the 'Connection' is created. This is for the "SDO_DIM_ELEMENT" type.
2) You can use the Query "SELECT diminfo from all_sdo_geom_metadata".
3) Use the "getVector" methods of the 'ResultSet' to retrieve a collection column:

vector<CSDODimElement*> v1; //SDO_DIM_ELEMENT = >CSDODimElement class
getVector(rs, 1, v1);

You can also check this posting:

http://forums.oracle.com/forums/thread.jspa?threadID=329030&tstart=0

Another suggestion is to do two changes to the compilation:

1) As noted elsewhere, use "/MD" verses "/MDd" compile switch.
2) Remove (undefined) "_DEBUG".

☞ **QUESTION 51**

OTT and setVector

I have a nested table where one of my columns is an object type.

> Type: attribute_t (id numvber, dataval varchar2(200)
> Type: attributes table of attribute_t
> Table: Objects (name varchar2(30), A Attributes)

I want an OCCI program that will populate the A column in the 'Objects table'.

Do I need to use OTT to define class types for the attributes column?

I ran OTT through specifying "a .typ" file of "case=lower" and "type attribute_t".

None of the resulting files from the OTT command produced any prototypes with a 'setVector' included.

What command should I use to get OTT to produce prototypes for 'setVector' and other 'set/get' methods?

✍ **ANSWER**

OTT generates the 'C++' class 'declaration/definition' for the object type "attribute_t". Assuming 'Objects' is a normal relational table, you need to do the following:

//attribute_t => CAttribute C++ class

```
vector<CAttribute *> vecobjs;

CAttribute *obj1 = new CAttribute();
//obj1->setId(), obj1->setDataval()... set the attributes
vecobjs.push_back(obj1);

CAttribute *obj2 = new CAttribute();
//obj2->setId(), obj2->setDataval()... set the attributes
vecobjs.push_back(obj2);

Statement    *conn->createStatement("insert    into    objects
values (:1,:2)");
setVector(stmt, 2, vecobjs, "USER", "ATTRIBUTE_T");
```

☞ QUESTION 52

dynamic array in "SetDataBuffer" function

The query is the following:

> string sqlStmt="select * from emp";

When I use a normal array, such as ": char output[8][100][20]" in "SetDataBuffer", the output is "[column][rownum][stringl en]", then the result is correct.

When I used a new query as follows:

```
char ***output = new char**[8];
for(int i=0; i<8; i++){
output = new char*[100];
for(int j=0; j<100){
output[j] = new char[20];
}
}
...
```

It can be compiled successfully, but got error in "setDataBuffer". I wrote a 'Pro*C' program and used a 'C' style dynamic malloc in array fetch, which also got an error.

How can I use a dynamic memory in OCCI?

Can I use this method in an OCI program instead?

✍ ANSWER

The memory must be continuous. The new example 'as static array output' "[8][100][20]". The dynamic is as follows:

```
char ***output = new char**[8];
for(int i=0; i<8; i++){
output = new char*[100];
output[0] = new char[20*100];
for(int j=1; j<100){
output[j] = output[j-1] + 20;
}
}
```

☞ QUESTION 53

To cancel a query in OCCI

The query are as follows:
1: ResultSet *rs = stmt->executeQuery();

2: while(rs->next (array_fetch_size))

For step 1 and step 2, in my application it will take a long time, maybe 10 min, to finish the OCCI calls. I tried to terminate the 'Environment' in another thread when it timed out, then I met the error. I tried then to cancel the thread, but it's also not a good idea.

Does anybody know the way to cancel a query or set a timeout parameter in OCCI call?

✍ ANSWER

You can use the method "getOCIServer" to get the OCI server handle. Then, use "OCIbreak" in the other thread. After that all OCI (and OCCI) call will be cancelled.

☞ QUESTION 54

OCCI & Signal Handling

Before calling any OCCI function, my signal handling (i.e. for SIGTERM) works. However, after calling OCCI 'environment/ connection', my signal handling did not worked. The OCCI version is 9.2.0.6.0.

It seems OCCI is 'stealing' my signals. Below is the basic test program:

The problem area: (c++)

```
oracle::occi::Environment *env;
oracle::occi::Connection *conn;
oracle::occi::Statement *stmt;
oracle::occi::ResultSet *rset;

::signal(SIGINT, signal_handle);
::signal(SIGTERM, signal_handle);
::signal(SIGPIPE, sigpipe_handle);

cout << "Attempting to connect to server" << endl;
try
{

env    =    oracle::occi::Environment::createEnvironment
(oracle::occi::Environment::DEFAULT);
conn = env->createConnection ("usr", "pswd", "db");

cout << "Connection Estabolished OK" << endl;

string sqlStmt = "SELECT I_STATUS FROM K_INC";
```

```
stmt = conn->createStatement (sqlStmt);
rset = stmt->executeQuery ();

while (rset->next ())
{
cout << "Result!" << rset->getString(1) << endl;
}

stmt->closeResultSet (rset);
conn->terminateStatement (stmt);
}
catch(oracle::occi::SQLException ex)
{
cout<<"Exception thrown for displayAllRows"<<endl;
cout><<"Error number: "<< ex.getErrorCode() << endl;
cout<<ex.getMessage() ><< endl;

cout << "We have a problem!" << endl;
}
```

Do you have an example of using signals with OCCI?

✍ ANSWER

There is no problem on signal stealing. You can use the signal handling before the connection, after the connection, and even after insertion of rows into the table. You can raise a signal in all the three cases and from another process using "kill -15 <process ID >" the signal handler seems to work fine.

The code is attached below, you can try it:

```
#include <iostream>
```

```
#include <occi.h>
#include<csignal>

using namespace oracle::occi;
using namespace std;
int i=1;
class occidml
{
private:

Environment *env;
Connection *conn;
Statement *stmt;
public:

occidml (string user, string passwd, string db)
{
env = Environment::createEnvironment (Environment::
DEFAULT);
conn = env->createConnection (user, passwd, db);
}

~occidml ()
{
env->terminateConnection (conn);
Environment::terminateEnvironment (env);
}

/**
* Inserting a row into the table.
*/
void insertRow ()
{
string sqlStmt = "INSERT INTO varun VALUES (111,
'ASHOK')";
```

```
stmt = conn->createStatement (sqlStmt);
try{
stmt->executeUpdate ();
cout << "insert - Success" << endl;
}catch(SQLException ex)
{
cout<<"Exception thrown for insertRow"<<endl;
cout><<"Error number: "<< ex.getErrorCode() << endl;
cout<<ex.getMessage() >« endl;
}

conn->terminateStatement (stmt);
}
};

void term(int sig)
{
cout << "handling signal no." << sig << endl;
i=i+1;
}

int main (void)
{
string user = "SCOTT";
string passwd = "TIGER";
string db = "";
signal(SIGTERM,term); // register a SIGTERM handler

while(i==1){}
printf("Before Connection\n");
occidml *demo = new occidml (user, passwd, db);

while (i==2){}
printf("After Connection\n");
cout << "Inserting a record into the table author_tab "
```

```
<<endl;
demo->insertRow ();
while(i==3){}
delete(demo);
printf("Complete");
}
```

☞ QUESTION 55

OCCI::Statement Native Syntax

With what language or syntax is an 'OCCI Statement' object created?

Is it set to Native?

✍ ANSWER

You can try the following:

```
Connection *conn = ...
...
Date d;
Statement *stmt = conn->createStatement();
string sql = "SELECT sysdate FROM dual";
stmt->setSQL(sql);
ResultSet *rs = stmt->executeQuery();
if (rs->next())
d = rs->getDate(1);
stmt->closeResultSet(rs);
conn->terminateStatement(stmt);
if (d.isNull())
{
cout << ":-(" << endl;
}
else
{
cout << ":-)" << endl;
}
```

☞ QUESTION 56

OCCI and Cygwin

While I could compile and run 'OCCI db application' in Windows, I couldn't get it run in Cygwin. The application is compiled in 'VC++'.

What can I do to make it run OCCI in cygwin?

✍ ANSWER

The application is compiled by 'cl' and link in 'VC++' (7.1). When running in Cygwin, it generates a bug-reporting error relevant to:

AppName: t.exe AppVer: 0.0.0.0 ModName: oranls10.dll
ModVer: 10.1.0.2 Offset: 000589e9

☞ QUESTION 57

MSVC Violation Access

I am using Oracle 10g. I am trying to run the 8-line example of OCCI. I am using Visual Studio.NET and was able to get the code to compile with the following settings:

Include Files:
%ORACLE HOME%\Db_1\OCI\include

Library Files:
%ORACLE HOME%\Db_1\OCI\lib\MSVC\vc71

In my 'link path', I have linked "oraocci10.lib". All of these are the files included with the Oracle 10g installation.

The problem is when I execute the program, the "env->createConnection(...);"
statement gives me a 'System Access Violation' exception.

I have tried the same settings except with the 'Instant Client LIB' and 'DLL files' with no success either.

How can I figure this out?

✍ ANSWER

You can solve this problem by just putting "oraocci10.dll" and "oci.dll" path to the head of "%PATH%". In Linux, there is no problem.

☞ QUESTION 58

refresh object

I select an object by 'value' (select value(i) ...) and do a "Abc
*obj = (Abc *)stmt->getObject(1)". Then I call the member
functions, and then delete the object "delete obj".

After some time, I called the same sequence of code with one
difference. The object was changed from another application.
The 'OCCI app' does not 'see' these changes, and I have to
restart it for the object changes to appear.

What is the correct way to force an update of the object in
the cache?

✍ ANSWER

Objects returned by "ResultSet::getObject()" are transient
objects, and are not managed by the object cache. Ensure
that you are re-executing the 'SELECT' query, and do a
"ResultSet::getObject" again. If serialized transactions are
being used, then a 'commit/rollback' needs to be done to see
the changes of another 'transaction/application'.

☞ QUESTION 59

getString VARCHAR2(200)

I have a table as follows:

T1(
id numeric,
name1 varchar2(50),
name2 varchar2(200)
)

When I select 'name1' all went well, but when 'name2' was elected, I got the 'Assertion':

File:dbgdel.cpp
Expression:BLOCK_TYPE_IS_VALID(pHead->nBlockUse)
Same memory allocation problem

My code is as follows:

```
Statement    *stmt    =    conn->createStatement("SELECT
name1,name2 from T1");
ResultSet *rs = stmt->executeQuery();
while(rs.next()){
string str1 = rs->getString(1);//All good
string str2 = rs->getString(2);//There assertion
}
```

I use 'VC71', Oracle Client 10 (oraocci10.dll, oraocci10.lib).

What can I do about this?

✍ ANSWER

If you are using MSVC's "/MDd" flag (debug C-Runtime libraries), then the application has to be linked with "oraocci10d.lib/oraocci10d.dll".

In Debug mode, you can use "oraocci10d.lib" with flag "/MDd". But in 'Release', if you use "oraocci10.lib", you will get the same error: "free.c ->HeapFree".

☞ QUESTION 60

Compilation error

I am getting a compilation error.

How can I find a guide to the complete steps, and a simple program of OCCI?

✍ ANSWER

You can check "occidml.cpp" under "%ORACLE_HOME%\rdbms\demo and make.bat" in the same directory on how to compile and link. In there, you will find the steps in compiling.

☞ QUESTION 61

OCCI environment

Where can I write OCCI programs and what files do I need for compilation?

How can I set and run a basic OCCI application?

✍ ANSWER

Here are steps you can take to correct the process:

1. You will need an 'Oracle Client installation' or 'Oracle Instant Client SDK' You can check the following website:

http://www.oracle.com/technology/software/tech/oci/instantclient/index.html

2. The OCCI header files are under "$ORACLE_HOME/rdbms/public (occi*.h)" (%ORACLE_HOME%/oci/include/ on Windows).

3. Check "$ORACLE_HOME/rdbms/demo/demo_rdbms.mk" or "%ORACLE_HOME%\rdbms\demo\make.bat" (Windows) on how to compile OCCI applications.

4. More information on OCCI can be found at:

http://www.oracle.com/technology/tech/oci/occi/index.html.

The Collateral section has a detailed OCCI training guide.

5. Check this post for more Windows specific information:
   http://forums.oracle.com/forums/thread.jsp?forum=168&th read=287460&tstart=0&trange=15

☞ QUESTION 62

Compiler Problems with Oracle 10

I developed an application using OCCI on Oracle 9i. As requested, I used the 'SUN FORTE WORKSHOP 6.2 C++ Compiler'. Now, my customer decided to go on Oracle 10.

If I try to compile and link the application with 'ORACLE 10', I get the following message: "Error Code 1: Input file / export/opt/SUNWspro/WS6U2/lib/drti.o". It contains a '32-bit relatable', but produced a '64-bit' file.

Do I need the 'SUN ONE Studio 8 C++ Compiler'?

✎ ANSWER

'Sun ONE Studio 8' will be required for creating '64-bit' OCCI applications. If you want to create a '32-bit' application, then you can check "$ORACLE_HOME/rdbms/demo/demo_ rdbms32.mk". The '32 bit libraries' are installed under "$ORCLE_HOME/rdbms/lib32".

☞ QUESTION 63

msvc++ 7.1

```
Try
{
conn = env->createConnection( username, password, db_
ident );
}
catch (SQLException &sqlExcp)
{
ErrorText = sqlExcp.what();
ErrorCode = sqlExcp.getErrorCode();
ConnectionOk = 0;
return ErrorCode;
}
catch (std::exception &excp)
{
ErrorText = excp.what();
ErrorCode = 1;
ConnectionOk = 0;
return ErrorCode;
}
catch ( ... )
{
ErrorText = "Unknown error connecting to oracle";
ErrorCode = 1;
ConnectionOk = 0;
return ErrorCode;
}
```

It works when I use my own PC, having a 10g client installed. But it doesn't work using 'instant client' on another pc. I use 'msvc++ 7.1'. In 'Debug mode', it works. I was able to connect and upload my data. In 'release mode', I got the "Unknown error connecting to Oracle", which means that I don't get a 'SQL exception' or a 'standard exception'.

Which catch-block should I include to get some more information on the exception that has occurred?

✍ ANSWER

Ensure that the correct 'MSVC 7.1' version of "oraocci10.dll" is first in the 'PATH'. An unknown exception indicates that a crash or access violation has occurred. You can use the "oraocci10.dll" that you can get from installing the 'instant client 10g', and use the one supplied in "oraclepath>\oci\lib\msvc\vc71" to solve the issue.

☞ QUESTION **64**

32bit libraries in Solaris 5.8

I have my earlier application built on 'Solaris 5.7', 'Oracle 8', and 'MQ 5.2' (all of them had 32bit libraries). Now, we are doing an upgrade. We have 'Solaris 5.8', 'Oracle 9.2', and 'MQ 5.3' (MQ has 32bit libs). I'm getting an error while trying to build due to this mismatch.

What can you suggest to fix this?

✍ ANSWER

Check "demo_rdbms32.mk" under "$ORACLE_HOME/ rdbms/demo". Oracle supplies '32-bit libraries' also (installed under "$ORACLE_HOME/rdbms/lib32").

☞ **QUESTION 65**

Exception ORA-32101 creating environment

I've got an "ORA-32101" exception creating environment with any parameters. (Environment *env = Environment:: createEnvironment();)

I am linking with the following libraries: 'libocci', 'liblnntsh', and 'libwtc9' using 'gcc 2.96' on 'rh72'. I have nothing but libraries from the oracle tools. I am compiling sample code and have "ORA-32101" exception creating environment with any applicable argument.

Do I need something more?

✍ **ANSWER**

This is a problem with libraries, and possibly other oracle installed was conflicting with the OCCI client. The OCCI client is designed to be 'thin' and "independent". But strangely, if it finds any spec of another oracle installed on the machine it, will try to use the "other" oracle libraries which results to failure of doing its process (incompatibilities showing up as "ORA-32101" errors). This is bad because your 'OCCI client libs' probably have a different version than what you have on your machine.

Setting "ORACLE_HOME" to a different 'install' of oracle doesn't stop it, because 'bad' libraries were still used. Your 'OCCI client libs' may try to use configuration files it finds under the "$ORACLE_HOME" tree (such as shretp.lst). You may get a really strange behavior.

You can do the following:

(1) Look in "ORACLE_HOME,LD_LIBRARY_PATH" or "SHLIB_PATH" for support 'libs' ('libsql' or whatever). If found, utilize these and any other supporting libraries and configuration files. You can completely ignore your 'OCCI libs' in the directory you unpacked them to.

(2) Look where you told them to search during 'linking phase' of build.

(3) Look in a search sequence (standard locations) for outstanding link items.

In other words, beware of any other oracle installed with environmental variables set to it (e.g. "ORACLE_HOME, LD_LIBRARY_PATH" or "SHLIB_PATH"), as this 'install/libs' will be used, and are probably completely incompatible with the OCCI client version you are using.

You can 'unset' "ORACLE_HOME" and add your own oracle 'OCCI client libs' to the "LD_LIBRARY_PATH" (on HPUX PA-RISC 32) before it would work.

☞ QUESTION **66**

executeArrayUpdate of objects

Is it possible to bulk inserting an array of simple objects (no nested objects or tables) directly, or do I have to build arrays of the attributes separately in order to execute the "executeArrayUpdate" function?

What type of macro is needed for objects to be able to make a call to "setDataBuffer"? (I.e. equivalent of 'OCCIINT' for array of integers is something like "OCCI_OBJECT)"?

✍ **ANSWER**

You cannot use "setDataBuffer" interface for objects. You can use "addIteration()/setObject()/execute()" methods.

☞ QUESTION **67**

OCCI vs. OCI

Which way is better for developing, OCI or OCCI?

✍ **ANSWER**

OCCI programs are shorter and much more readable than equivalent OCI programs. But you can only use OCCI with a 'C++' compiler, and not a plain 'C' compiler. With OCI, you can use either 'C' or 'C++'.

☞ QUESTION 68

OCI and PL/SQL

We are using 'PL/SQl' predominantly in our application, which is an 'OLTP' application. We need our responses to be sub second. We were checking if OCI embedded in 'C' would give us any performance improvement over 'PL/SQL', as one of our customers wants to do '4000 TPM'.

Can we execute this?

✍ ANSWER

You first have to profile your existing application to see where the bottlenecks are, before you can make any decisions on tuning performance. If the application is 'server side data intensive', then moving the data access to the client (and away from the data) will probably only slow things down.

There are also other alternatives such as 'PL/SQL' native compilation.

☞ QUESTION 69

OCIHandleFree method

I have two methods as stated below:

```
A::openConnection()
{
...
occiConn = occiEnv->createConnection(...);
ociEnv = occiEnv->getOCIEnvironment();
ociSvcCtx = occiConn->getOCIServiceContext();
...
OCIHandleAlloc(ociEnv, (void**)&ociError, OCI_HTYPE_
ERROR, 0, NULL));

OCIHandleAlloc(ociEnv, (void**)&oci_transaction, OCI_
HTYPE_TRANS, 0, 0));

OCIAttrSet(ociSvcCtx, OCI_HTYPE_SVCCTX, oci_
transaction, 0, OCI_ATTR_TRANS, ociError));
...
}

A::closeConnection()
{
...
OCIHandleFree(oci_transaction, OCI_HTYPE_TRANS));
OCIHandleFree(ociError, OCI_HTYPE_ERROR));

occiEnv->terminateConnection(occiConn);
...
}
```

My program in UNIX (Sun OS) creates connection by calling the "openConnection()" method, and sends some SQL requests. If the request can't be treated (for example: due to the locked record in the DB), the program tries to re-establish connection by calling the "closeConnection()" method, and after some delay the "openConnection()" one. In this case, my program core dumped in the "occiEnv->terminateConnection()" method, or in the "occiEnv->createConnection()" one. If I add some delay (some unuseful code) after freeing the transaction handle (closeConnection() method), the program will work well.

I suggested that the "OCIHandleFree()" function only starts some thread which really frees the transaction handle. When the "occiEnv->terminateConnection()" method was called, the thread is still freeing the transaction handle.

What can be the cause of such behavior?

✍ ANSWER

Make sure that you have cleared the transaction handle from the service context before the "OCIHandleFree" (HTYPE_TRANS) and "terminateConnection()". Or you can free the transaction handle after the connection is terminated.

☞ QUESTION **70**

OCCI and Statement Caching

I am plotting a strategy for porting our application servers to Oracle using OCCI, and I am looking for practice information. So far, I found a clean fit using "StatelessConnectionPool".

I read an OCCI performance white paper that recommended using "Statement::setSQL()" rather than creating a new 'Statement' each time. But I also read about a statement caching in the 10g docs.

Does "setSQL()" bypass the statement cache, or worse, defeat it?

The application server dynamically generates nearly all of its SQL. However, through the use of bind variables, the overall number of SQL statements is not large. A small number of statements constitute 90% of the statements executed. A statement cache of 20 or so would probably serve me quite well.

Rather than using "setSQL()", would it be better to use "Connection::createStatement()", betting that the statement is cached?

The description of "Connection::terminateStatement()" is scant. Do I have to pass a key to terminate "Statement()", and to have the statement cached rather than destroyed? If so, can the key be the SQL text itself?

✍ Answer

"Statement::setSQL()" can be used to save on 'Statement' handle/object allocation costs. It does not bypass the 'Statement' cache, nor does any 'Statement' caching.

It is true that the statement cache will be used whether you use "setSQL()" or always do a "createStatement". If you are going to do a "createStatement()", process the 'resultset', close the 'resultset', terminate 'Statement' and create the next statement, if all these are done in order, then, you can just have one statement and do "setSQL()" whenever you want to execute a new statement. It will still use the statement caching underneath.

If you are going to operate on multiple 'resultsets' at the same time, you should have separate statements. This model too makes use of statement caching. You can do with what fits your statement processing logic.

Passing a tag is not mandatory. The statements will still be cached. The sql text itself serves as the default key. The user can give a tag while terminating the statement, just to group that statement along with other statements of the same tag. This tag will serve as the key when a "createStatement()" is called with that tag (a bit faster than using the sql text as the key).

☞ QUESTION 71

OCI-21500 segmentation fault 'RefImpl'

Assigning the result of persistent new 'T' to 'Ref<T>' segmentation faults with stack trace, and my debugger shows it to be in the 'Ref<T>' class on a line instating "RefImpl(PObject *)".

Is there a solution for this?

✍ ANSWER

It is a known bug and Oracle is working on it. It occurs only when you are trying to get a 'Ref' from a new object being made persistent using a view. You can workaround by committing the new object, and re-querying for getting the 'Ref' of it.

☞ QUESTION 72

debug version of OCCI 9 lib/dll

I am working on a 'Win32' application with MSVC 6.0. The release builds work, but the debug version crashes. For OCCI 10g, I can see two sets of 'dll' and 'libs'. But for OCCI 9, there is only release version. (I downloaded 9i client)

How can I get the debug version?

✍ ANSWER

You can link "MSVCRT.DLL" instead of "MSVCRTD.DLL" like this:

cl -GX -DWIN32COMMON -I. -If:\oracle920\oci\include -Id:\PROGRA~1\MICROS~1\vc98\include -I. -D_DLL -D_MT test.cpp /link /LIBPATH:f:\oracle920\oci\lib\msvc /LIBPATH:d:\PROGRA~1\MICROS~1\vc98\lib

oci.lib msvcrt.lib msvcprt.lib oraocci9.lib /nod:libc

Or, you can make sure that "msvcprt.lib" is included like this:

cl -GX -DWIN32COMMON -I. -If:\oracle920\oci\include -Id:\PROGRA~1\MICROS~1\vc98\include -I. -D_DLL -D_MT test.cpp /link /LIBPATH:f:\oracle920\oci\lib\msvc /LIBPATH:d:\PROGRA~1\MICROS~1\vc98\lib oci.lib msvcrtd.lib msvcprt.lib oraocci9.lib /nod:libc

The IDE defaults to use the "/MDd" switch, and leaves out the "msvcprt.lib".

Another suggestion is to remove "_DEBUG" from your compiler setting, because of the different implementation of 'delete' in "msvcrt.dll" and "msvcrtd.dll".
The OCCI libraries override the default implementation of new operators, and delete the part of 'the' problem when linking in the default libraries in a debug mode.

☞ QUESTION 73

OTT and ORACLE_HOME

I installed oracle default, and its environment name is "ORACLE_HOME1". When I run 'OTT', it stated "ORACLE_HOME:not defined". Then I set the "ORACLE_HOME" and related "CLASSPATH", and run OTT again. But I got the exception about "can't locate the function 'kpuhhalo' input point in oci.dll".

How can I correct it?

✍ ANSWER

Make certain that "%ORACLE_HOME%\bin" is present in your 'PATH' environment variable.

☞ Question 74

Steps on using OCCI

What are the steps of creating a windows application, and a windows 'dll'?

I'm using the system windows server 2003, VS.Net 2003, and Oracle 10g.

✍ Answer

You can do the following:

1) Set Visual C++'s 'INCLUDE' setting to have the location of the OCCI header files: "%ORACLE_HOME%\oci\include", "LIB" setting to have the location of "OCCI vc71 libraries : %ORACLE_HOME%\oci\lib\msvc\vc71".

2) Include "occi.h" in your source.

3) Add "oraocci10.lib" in your "application/dll" link line.

☞ QUESTION 75

Updating a DATE value

I need to update a record which has a 'DATE', 'NUMBER', and 'VARCHAR2' attributes. In the application, I wish to create a SQL statement like: "UPDATE table SET date='20052903' WHERE attr = 'example'", and run this with "executeUpdate".

I can't use the "to_date('20052903', 'YYYYMMDD')". I have to make the format 'valid'. I need to change the 'NLS' within my application.

How can I do this?

How can I set the Format 'YYYYMMDD' valid for the update?

✍ ANSWER

For the date value '20052903', the format needs to be 'YYYYDDMM'. Before running the inserts or updates, execute:

    alter session set nls_date_format = 'YYYYDDDMM';

☞ QUESTION 76

getNumArrayRows( ) and next(N)

My oracle version is 9.2. First, I patched it to '9.2.0.5.0', and used OCCI to interact with it. "occi::ResultSet:: getNumArrayRows()" returned the total number of fetched rows until "occi::ResultSet::next(N)" was last invoked. For example: I fetched 'next(1000)' successfully for two times, then "getNumArrayRows()" returned 2000.

But after I patched it to '9.2.0.6.0', the "getNumArrayRows()" behaved different, it returned the number of rows that was last fetched. E.g. was same with above operation, "getNumArrayRows()" returned 1000.

In addition, "occi::ResultSet::next(N)" also behaved differently. In '9.2.0.5.0', if "ResultSet::next(1000)" and actual rows in tables is 500, the return value equals "END_OF_ FETCH", but in '9.2.0.6.0', it was "DATA_AVAILABLE".

How different is '9.2.0.6' from '9.2.0.5' in 'OCCI API'?

✍ ANSWER

What you are experiencing now is the correct behavior. It was a problem that is fixed in '9.2.0.6'. "getNumArrayRow()" returns the actual number of rows fetched in the last call to 'next()'. 'next()' returns "DATA_AVAILABLE" as long as "getNumArrayRows()" is more than 0. It is easier to program this way and in line with the documentation.

You should also take note that "getNumArrayRows()" is applicable only when "rset->next()" returns "DATA_ AVAILABLE".

☞ QUESTION 77

IN/OUT Parameter

I don't know what's wrong with OCCI 10g Instant Client. I tried to call a procedure and a function, and then I could not get the correct result. It seems my parameter doesn't work. My platform is Win2K (VC++6) and HP-UX (aCC).

The following is the test result:

callfun - invoking a PL/SQL function having IN, IN/OUT and IN/OUT parameters
Executing the block :BEGIN :1 := demo_fun (:2, :3, :4); END;
Update Count : 1
Printing the INOUT & INOUT parameters:
ret = 10
v2 = ?? .... >> Expect to be "[IN-OUT_1]"!!
v3 = col1=[10], col2=[IN-OUT_1]
occiproc - done

The following is the function:

CREATE OR REPLACE FUNCTION demo_fun (col1 IN NUMBER, col2 IN OUT VARCHAR2,
col3 IN OUT VARCHAR2) RETURN INTEGER AS
temp VARCHAR2(100);
BEGIN
temp := col3;
col3 := 'col1=[' || col1 || '], col2=[' || col2 || ']' ;
col2 := temp;
RETURN col1;
END;

/

The following is the OCCI code:

```
try
{
cout << "callfun - invoking a PL/SQL function having IN, IN/
OUT and IN/OUT ";
cout << "parameters" << endl;
Statement *stmt = conn->createStatement("BEGIN :1 :=
demo_fun (:2, :3, :4); END;");
cout << "Executing the block :" << stmt->getSQL() << endl;

stmt->registerOutParam (1, OCCIINT);
stmt->setInt (2, 10);
stmt->setString (3, "IN-OUT_1");
stmt->setString (4, "IN-OUT_2");
stmt->registerOutParam(4, OCCISTRING, 100);

int updateCount = stmt->executeUpdate ();
cout << "Update Count : " << updateCount << endl;

cout << "Printing the INOUT & INOUT parameters:" <<
endl;
cout << "ret = " << stmt->getInt (1) << endl;
cout << "v2 = " << stmt->getString (3) << endl;
cout << "v3 = " << stmt->getString (4) << endl;

conn->terminateStatement (stmt);
cout << "occiproc - done" << endl;
}
catch(SQLException ex)
{
cout<<"Exception thrown for executeQuery"<<endl;
cout><<"Error number: "<< ex.getErrorCode() << endl;
```

```
cout<<ex.getMessage() ><< endl;
}
```

As quoted from the OCCI programming guide "...if there is an 'IN/OUT' parameter, then just use "setXXX()" and "getXXX()" without "registerOutParam()"." Is it true?

When I ignore "registerOutParam()", I will get an exception as below:

Error number: 6502
ORA-06502: PL/SQL: numeric or value error
ORA-06512: at "ESMS.DEMO_FUN", line 6
ORA-06512: at line 1

What else can I use to correct this?

✍ ANSWER

You can use "setMaxParamSize" on the statement before you do a "setString(4, "IN-OUT_2")". "registerOutParam" must be called for out parameters only. "setxxx()" methods are used for 'in/out' parameters.

You can try the following:

```
stmt->registerOutParam (1, OCCIINT);
stmt->setInt (2, 10);
stmt->setString (3, "IN-OUT_1");
stmt->setMaxParamSize(4,100);
stmt->setString (4, "IN-OUT_2");
//stmt->registerOutParam(4, OCCISTRING, 100);
```

☞ QUESTION 78

OCCI call PL/SQL Procedure with 2 IN/OUT Parameters

I encountered a problem with OCCI when I called a procedure with two 'IN/OUT' parameters. I got an error (core dump).

CREATE OR REPLACE PROCEDURE demo_proc (v1 in integer, v2 in out
    varchar2, v3 in out varchar2);

The OCCI code as follows:
```
stmt = conn->createStatement
("BEGIN demo_proc(:v1, :v2, :v3); END;");
cout << "Executing the block :" << stmt->getSQL() << endl;
stmt->setInt (1, 10);
stmt->setString (2, "Test1");
stmt->setString (3, "First");
int updateCount = stmt->executeUpdate ();
cout << "Update Count:" << updateCount << endl;

cout << "Printing the INOUT & OUT parameters:" << endl;
string c1 = stmt->getString (2);
cout << c1 << endl;
string c2 = stmt->getString (3);
```

When I run the result, I got the following: Bus error(coredump)

But If I get just only one of string from 'v1' or 'v2', I will get the correct result.

How can I avoid this two 'IN/OUT' parameters issue?

✍ ANSWER

The root cause might seem very strange in initializing the environment variable.

```
=== FAILED ===
Environment *env;
=== SUCCESS ===
Environment *env = NULL;

cout << "occidml - createEnvironment" << endl;
env = Environment::createEnvironment (Environment::
OBJECT);
```

You can fix this issue in 'Win2K' and 'HP-UX 11'.

☞ QUESTION 79

ORA-06521: PL/SQL: Error mapping function

I am getting this error after binding and searching an 'ldap' directory:

ORA-06521: PL/SQL: Error mapping function
ORA-06512: at "SYS.DBMS_LDAP_API_FFI", line 0
ORA-06512: at "SYS.DBMS_LDAP", line 1338
ORA-06512: at "SYS.DBMS_LDAP", line 1273
ORA-06512: at "SYS.DBMS_LDAP", line 529
ORA-06512: at line 127

Line 127 is:
my_dn:= DBMS_LDAP.get_dn(my_session, my_entry);

Both of the 'my_...' parameters have been successfully set earlier in the script, as they did not produce any errors and "DBMS_LDAP.count_entries(my_session,   my_message)" returns = 1.

I followed the example at:
http://download-west.oracle.com/docs/cd/B10501_01/
network.920/a96577/smplcode.htm#636994

Any of the functions used in the 'while loop' in the above example, gave a similar error, (and get same errors if I move them out of the loop).

Apparently "SYS.DBMS_LDAP_API_FFI" is a call to an external 'C' program, but this would be a standard Oracle one, not the one I have written. I am connected to a non-Oracle 'ldap' server, and have tried several "OpenLDAP 2.X, & Windows 2000 AD", but got the same results.

How can I resolve this issue?

✍ ANSWER

You can fix it by running the 'catldap.sql' script "ORACLE_HOME/rdbms/admin/catldap.sql" as 'SYS' user, and re-create the "dbms_ldap" packages.

☞ QUESTION 80

Fetching more than one row at a time

I have a sample code given in the documentation (listed below). It throws a data truncated exception on the employee number (even if the field has only 4 digits).

```
int empno[5];
char ename[5][11];
ub2 enameLen[5];
ResultSet *resultSet = stmt->executeQuery("select empno, ename from emp");
resultSet->setDataBuffer(1, &empno, OCCIINT);
resultSet->setDataBuffer(2, ename, OCCI_SQLT_STR, sizeof(ename[0]), enameLen);
rs->next(5); // throws ORA-01406!
```

Is there a solution to this problem?

✎ ANSWER

You should pass the size of the number field too. Use:

```
"resultSet->setDataBuffer(1, empno, OCCIINT, sizeof(empno[0]))";
```

☞ QUESTION 81

OCCI and OTT, a serious technology

I have been evaluating 'OCCI/OTT' coming from a 'Pro*C' background, and standing on the eve of re-engineering a large enterprise class software system. It is a very serious decision for us to make a transition to 'OCCI/OTT' away from 'Pro*C'. The reason we are even contemplating it is the potential for a more development process, given an 'OO' design methodology and 'UML' documentation. I struggled however to be convinced that the 'OTT/OCCI' combination is a serious development technology mainly due to 'patchy' documentation when it comes to anything exceeding the basic (especially OTT), and stability when it comes to multi-threading.

Could you provide an opinion whether it would be worth my while to continue investigating or rather steer clear?

✍ ANSWER

It certainly is a serious technology, if by serious you mean that Oracle is committed to developing and extending it, and it is intended for production use.

It is a 'new' API, and hence not as well documented or quite as thoroughly fleshed out as say 'Pro*C' or 'OCI' (both of which have been around for decades). Each release (9, 9i R2, 10g, 10g R2) has continued to improve in all of these areas.

☞ Question 82

Entry point of procedure "xaoSvcCtx" not found

I wrote the following program:

```
#include "stdafx.h"
#include <occi.h>
using namespace oracle::occi;
using namespace std;
int _tmain(int argc, _TCHAR* argv[])
{
Environment *env;
Connection *conn;
Statement *stmt;

env = Environment::createEnvironment (Environment::
DEFAULT);
conn = env->createConnection("user", "password", "testd");

string sqlStmt = "SELECT n_ldg_id, name FROM test950";
stmt = conn->createStatement (sqlStmt);
ResultSet *rset = stmt->executeQuery ();

try
{
while (rset->next ())
{
cout << "n_ldg_id: " << rset->getString(1);
cout << rset->getString (2) << endl;
}
```

```
stmt->closeResultSet (rset);
conn->terminateStatement (stmt);
}catch(SQLException ex)
{
cout<<"Exception thrown for displayAllRows"<<endl;
cout><<"Error number: "<< ex.getErrorCode() << endl;
cout<<ex.getMessage() ><< endl;
}

return 0;


}
```

This are my settings in VC++ 7.1:
include files:
C:\oracle\product\10.1.0\Client_1\oci\include

library files :
C:\oracle\product\10.1.0\Client_1\oci\lib\msvc\vc71
linker/input
additional library:
oraocci10.lib

In 'windows\system32', I copied the file "oraocci10.dll".

The program compiled and linked fine. But when I run it, I got:

"The procedure's entry point is not found in the link library oci.dll"

Why did I get this message?

✍ **ANSWER**

Don't copy files from the 'Oracle Home\bin directory'. They are there because Oracle expects them to be and Oracle will version and update them with the installer. If you relocate them, then this entire mechanism gets broken.

As you have found out, the Oracle client is more than a single 'DLL'. Make sure the 'Oracle client' is installed, and that the "oracle home\bin directory" is in the 'OS' search path.

☞ **QUESTION 83**

Borland C++ Builder 6

Is it true that OCCI does not support 'Borland C++ Builder 6'?

✍ **ANSWER**

Oracle doesn't provide 'C++' class libraries that use Borland name mangling. Add that to the fact that Borland uses 'OMF' format for libraries and 'MS' uses 'COFF'. Oracle only supplies 'COFF'.

☞ QUESTION 84

Use OCCI to retrieve info

I used OCCI to retrieve information, but now I need to insert a row. But I keep getting a "core dump".

This is how I do a retrieve:

```
ResultSet *rset;
string sqlStmt = "SELECT STYLE,SIZE_DESC, SKU_DESC
FROM ITEM_MASTER WHERE SKU_ID = :1";
string parm(id);
string style="",size="",desc="";
stmt = conn->createStatement (sqlStmt);
try{
stmt->setString(1, parm);
rset = stmt->executeQuery();
}
catch( SQLException ex )
{
cout << "Exception thrown"<<"\r\n";
cout << "Error nÃºmer: "<<ex.getErrorCode()><<"\r\n";
cout << ex.getMessage() << "\r\n";
}
try{
if(rset->next())
{
style = rset->getString(1);
size = rset->getString(2);
desc = rset->getString(3);
}
}
catch(SQLException ex)
```

```
{
cout << "Exception thrown"<<"\r\n";
cout << "Error nÃºmer: "<<ex.getErrorCode()><<"\r\n";
cout << ex.getMessage()<<"\r\n";
}
stmt->closeResultSet(rset);
```

Then, I tried to insert like this:

```
int count=0;
string sqlStmt = "INSERT INTO XREF (CO,DIV,VENDOR_
BRCD,SKU_BRCD,SCAN_QNTY,CREATE_DATE_
TIME,USER_ID)   VALUES   ('SAM','SAM',:1,:2,:3,(SELECT
SYSDATE FROM DUAL),'BK')";
string parm1(vendor_brcd);
string parm2(barcode);
stmt->setAutoCommit(true);
stmt = conn->createStatement (sqlStmt);
try{
stmt->setString(1, parm1);
stmt->setString(2, parm2);
stmt->setInt(3, fjoldi);
count = stmt->executeUpdate();
if( count > 0 )
{
successful = true;
}
}
catch( SQLException ex )
{
cout << "Exception thrown"<<"\r\n";
cout << "Error nÃºmer: "<<ex.getErrorCode()><<"\r\n";
cout << ex.getMessage() << "\r\n";
}
stmt->setAutoCommit(false);
```

What did I do wrong?s

✍ ANSWER

The code looks okay. You can also check the 'stack trace'. Also check if there is a valid 'Statement handle' at this point:

```
stmt->setAutoCommit(true);
```

If the 'Commit' is not executed, you can put a 'manual commit' in there.

☞ **QUESTION 85**

NULL in OCCI

How can I pass 'null values' in the following code?

```
unsigned int v = 0;
iStmt = iConn->createStatement("INSERT INTO CONDITIONS
(Value) VALUES (:1)");
iStmt->setUInt(1, v); // here!!!
iStmt->executeUpdate();
iConn->commit();
iConn->terminateStatement(iStmt);
```

✍ **ANSWER**

You can try the following:

```
iStmt->setNull(1, OCCINUMBER); //
```

☞ QUESTION 86

Setting Transaction Isolation

Is there an 'OCCI API' to set the transaction isolation level for a connection? (e.g. "TRANSACTION_READ_COMMITTED", "TRANSACTION_SERIALIZABLE", etc)

✍ ANSWER

There is no API, you have to execute the corresponding SQL statements through "Statement::execute":

    stmt->execute("SET TRANSACTION ISOLATION LEVEL SERIALIZABLE");

☞ **QUESTION 87**

"OCIEnvNlsCreate"

I created a 'UNICODE' database using the database configuration assistant and wrote a 'UNICODE' application. Unfortunately, I fell over at the first hurdle. "OCIEnvNlsCreate" returns "OCI_ERROR" every time.

status = OCIEnvNlsCreate((OCIEnv **)&envhp, 0, 0, 0, 0, 0, 0, 0, OCI_UTF16ID, OCI_UTF16ID);

In order to use "OCIEnvNlsCreate", "NLS_LANG" and "NLS_NCHAR" can't have a 'UTF-16 setting'.

I can use "OCIEnvCreate" to obtain an environment handle, but then "OCILogon" fails if I pass a wide character strings for username and password etc. TNS can't resolve the server name. I can convert the strings to 'mbc' strings, but does this mean that I would have to do this for all strings I 'read/write' 'from/to' the database?

What can be the explanation for this?

✍ **ANSWER**

The two parameters to "OCIEnvNlsCreate" are 'charset' and 'ncharset'. If "OCI_UTF16ID" is passed for 'charset', then all 'usernames/passwords/object names/SQL text/TNS' and data for all "CHAR/VARCHAR2" columns must be in a "UTF16 characterset". If "OCI_UTF16ID" is passed for 'ncharset' parameter, then data for "NCHAR/NVARCHAR2" columns must be in 'UTF16'.

☞ QUESTION 88

OTT and backup files

OTT in a 10.2 environment seems to make backup copies of existing output files. If one of my generated output files is "XXX.cpp" and I run OTT two times, I will get "XXX.cpp" and "XXX.cpporcl".

Is there a parameter to switch off this behavior?

✍ ANSWER

On Linux, you can try to run it like this:

```
$ ls
in.typ

$ cat in.typ
MAPFILE=xm.cpp
TYPE typ AS Test

$ ott userid=scott/tiger code=cpp attraccess=private
cppfile=a.cpp hfile=a.h intype=in.typ outtype=out.typ use_
marker=true

$ ls *cpp*
a.cpp xm.cpp

$ ott userid=scott/tiger code=cpp attraccess=private
```

cppfile=a.cpp hfile=a.h intype=in.typ outtype=out.typ use_
marker=true

$ ls *cpp*

a.cpp xm.cpp

Also check the platform you are on.

☞ Question 89

new problem in XP service pack 2, vc7.1

Is the following code ok?

```
sql_sel_zqdm = "SELECT zqdm,zqjg FROM xt_ywzqfz
WHERE ywxh == :x ";
try{
stmt = conn->createStatement(sql_sel_zqdm);
stmt->setString(1,"123456789");
ResultSet *rset = stmt->executeQuery();
while( rset->next()){
string zqdm = rset->getString(1) ;
double zqjg = rset->getDouble(2);
}
}catch(SQLException s){
cerr << s.getErrorCode() << " " << s.getMessage() << endl;
}
```

When I run these codes, the "stmt->setString()" didn't work. When I get string from "stmt->getString()", the return string will cause 'debug assert'. I trace into "xstring" file of 'ms std lib', it stated "_block_type_is_valid(pHead->nBlockUse)".

What is the cause of this problem?

✍ Answer

For the 'debug assert' problem, you need to use the debug CRT flag '/MDd' of VC++, then link with "oraocci10d.lib" (VC++ 7.1 version).

Also replace the "==" in the SELECT with a single "=".

☞ QUESTION 90

connect string

I'm on Oracle 9.2. If I want to connect to a remote database, how can I construct the 'connectString' for "env->connect()"? Let's say the service name is A.B and the port # is 1234 (not the default 1521).

✍ ANSWER

You can either use a TNS alias as defined in your "TNSNAMES. ORA", or you can use the entire TNS 'Name-value' pair:

```
(DESCRIPTION =
(ADDRESS_LIST =
(ADDRESS  =  (PROTOCOL  =  TCP)(HOST  =  myhost.
org)(PORT = 1234))
)
(CONNECT_DATA =
(SERVER = DEDICATED)
(SERVICE_NAME = A.B)
)
)
```

Substitute your host name and IP address as appropriate.

☞ QUESTION 91

Date objects, setDataBufferArray, executeUpdate

I like to be able to set up an array of date objects together with a null indicator arrays and length arrays. And then, call "setDataBufferArray" followed by "executeUpdate". However, if I specify that the type is 'OCCIDATE', it throws an exception in 'tbe' "setDataBufferArray" call, and if I specify "OCCI_SQLT_DATE", it blows up in "executeUpdate".

This is a brief summary of the code:

```
m_pEnv = Environment::createEnvironment
(Environment::OBJECT);
pConn = m_pEnv->createConnection
(sName, sPassword, sConnectString);
pStmt = pConn->createStatement
("BEGIN Insert_Date_Types(:1); END;");

// Set data into an array of date types
// Set array of lengths to sizeof(date)
// Set array of indicators to all 0

pStmt->setDataBufferArray
(
1, // Which parameter this is
(void*)m_pData, // Where the data is
OCCI_SQLT_DATE, // DataType (OCCIDATE?)
nMaxDataValues, // Max number of elements
&nActualDataValues,// Actual number of elements
sizeof(Date), // Size of each element
```

pDataElementLengths, // Element lengths
pInds, // Null indicators
0 // Return codes: unused
);
pStmt->executeUpdate();

Is it possible to send an array or a table of 'date types' to the database?

✍ ANSWER

You are correct in using "OCCI_SQLT_DATE", but the 'date array' which goes in should be an array of 'OCIDate' rather than 'OCCI Date objects'.
The OCCI document is not very clear on this though.

☞ QUESTION 92

OCCI on Borland C++ Builder 6

[Linker Error] Unresolved external 'oracle::occi::
Environment::createEnvironment(oracle::occi::
Environment::Mode, void *, void * (*)(void *, unsigned int),
void * (*)(void *, void *, unsigned int), void (*)(void *, void
*))' referenced from D:\WORK\OCCIBCBTEST\UNIT1.OBJ

The above error is 'compile c++build6' code. I used
'c++builder6' "implib.exe" 'lib oraocci9.lib' from "oraocci9.
dll". Is this the right way?

But 'c++builder' "coff2omf.exe" is not 'lib include c++ LIB to
c++builder6's LIB'.

What can be the reason for this?

✍ ANSWER

'Borland C++' is not supported for OCCI on Windows.
Microsoft Visual C++ 6.0, 7.0 & 7.1 are the supported
compilers.

☞ QUESTION 93

"createConnection" crashes with 10g & VC 6 and VC 7.1

I tried all the switches in VC 7.1 and VC 6 (/ML, /MD, etc) in sequence, in either debug or release, using the proper version of the library (oraocci10.lib or oraocci10d.lib). I am using the sample program "occistre.cpp" connecting to 10g. All crashed with an: "Access violation reading location 0x00385000".

Can I get an execution that will work properly on 10g?

✍ ANSWER

You can check which "oraocci10.dll" is first in the 'PATH'. The "oraocci10.dll" under "%ORACLE_HOME%\bin" is the 'VC6' version. You have to use "/MD" to link with "oraocci10. lib/dll" and "/MDd" (debug CRT) to link with "oraocci10d. lib/dll"

☞ Question 94

Environment Class

When I call:

env=Environment::createEnvironment   (Environment::
DEFAULT);

I get the message:

error LNK2019: Not resolved extern Symbol '"public: static
class oracle::occi::Environment *

The usual '#includes' are made:

#include "stdafx.h"

#include <iostream>
#include <occi.h>
using namespace oracle::occi;
using namespace std;

I am working on 'Visual C++ Net', Windows XP.

In which library or header file is the 'Environment class'
defined?

✍ Answer

'VC++ 7.0' (.NET 2002) is supported in the 9.2.0.5 patch
set. 'VC++ 7.1' (.NET 2003) is supported with the 10gR1

release. The application should be linked with "oraocci9. lib/oraocci10.lib" present under "%ORACLE_HOME%\ rdbms\lib\vc7" or "%ORACLE_HOME%\rdbms\lib\vc71". The appropriate "oraocci.dll" should be first in the 'PATH' when running the application.

☞ QUESTION 95

The size of an OCCI "ResultSet"

Is there a method that returns the number of rows in a "ResultSet"?

✍ ANSWER

No. Oracle itself doesn't know how many rows will be returned until the last row is returned. You could add a "count(*)" to your query, and/or fetch all the rows if you really need a precise count of the rows.

☞ QUESTION 96

Error ORA 32103 with CLOB and utf8

From the following code, I got error "ORA 32103" when reading from 'CLOB', when the "NLS_LANG" environment variable is set to "american_america.AL32UTF8" or "american_america. UTF8".

If it is "american_america.we8iso8859p1", it works.
The client platform is "uname –a
HP-UX saelnk10 B.11.00 U 9000/800 687309392" unlimited user license.
The Oracle server is win2000, and the Oracle version in both platforms is 9.2.0.4.

oerr ora 32103
32103, 00000, "error from OCI call"
// *Cause: An error code other than OCI_ERROR is returned from an OCI call.
// *Action: This is an internal OCCI Error. Please contact customer support.

Here is the code:
```
while(rset->next())
{
for(int i=1 ; i <= colCount; ++i){
std::string colName = mdata[i-1].getString(MetaData::ATTR_
NAME);
std::string colValue;

if(mdata[i-1].getInt(MetaData::ATTR_DATA_TYPE) == OCCI_
SQLT_CLOB)
{
```

```
Clob clob = rset->getClob(i);
if(!clob.isNull()){
unsigned int cloblen = clob.length();
if (cloblen > 0){
char *buffer = new char[cloblen+1];
clob.open(OCCI_LOB_READONLY);
unsigned int chars = clob.read(cloblen, (unsigned char*)buffer,
cloblen+1);
// here in clob.read comes the ora-32103
```

So where's the customer support?

✍ ANSWER

If the client character set is 'UTF8', then the 'bufsize' parameter to the "Clob::read()" call must be at least 3 times the amt parameter, even if there are only single byte characters in the 'CLOB'.

```
//max character size in UTF8 = 3 bytes
char *buffer = new char[cloblen*3];
unsigned int chars =
clob.read(cloblen, (unsigned char*)buffer, cloblen*3);
```

☞ QUESTION 97

BLOB vs. OCCI_BLOB

I read in the OCCI programmer's guide that "setDataBuffer()" can be used instead of "setXXX()" for better performance. The following is their code example:

```
stmt ->setSQL("insert into emp (id, ename) values (:1, :2)");
char enames[2][] = {"SMITH", "MARTIN"};
ub2 enameLen[2];
for (int i = 0; i < 2; i++)
enameLen = strlen(enames + 1);
int ids[2] = {7369, 7654};
ub2 idLen[2] = {sizeof(ids[0], sizeof(ids[1])};
stmt->setDataBuffer(1,   ids,   OCCIINT,   sizeof(ids[0]),
&idLen);
stmt->setDataBuffer(2,      enames,      OCCI_SQLT_STR,
sizeof(ename[0]), &len);
stmt->executeArrayUpdate(2); // data for two rows is
inserted.
```

According to 'BLOB', "setDataBuffer()" only supports "OCCI_SQLT_BLOB" (which maps to 'C++' type "LNOCILobLocator"). However, the documentation later only describes "OCCIBLOB" (which maps to 'C++' "datatype" Blob). "OCCIBLOB" appears to be an OCCI class, but "OCCI_SQLT_BLOB" is not?

Can I use an "LNOCILobLocator" in my 'C++' code, or is better to stick with the OCCI classes? Where exactly does this "LNOCILobLocator" come from?

✍ Answer

"setDataBuffer" is beneficial if you have too much of string data, to avoid multiple copies and 'STL' string instantiation. It is OCI interface embedded in an OCCI program.

For 'Blobs', it doesn't make much of a difference. You can use "setMaxIterations", "setClob/addIteration", and "executeUpdate" methods.

☞ Question 98

Oracle session

I programmed a demo with OCCI and "connectionpool". After "connectionpool" was created, I found two sessions in the oracle database. I created a connection with the "connectionpool", and then found three sessions in the database.

Why was the new 3rd session was not used to create sessions?

✍ Answer

The sessions that are created when you create the pool, are internal sessions used for multiplexing of connections. They are not user sessions.

☞ QUESTION 99

Connect Pool

ConnectionPool *connPool = env->createConnectionPool
(poolUserName, poolPassword, connectString, 1, 5, 1);
Connection   *conn1   =   connPool->createConnection
(username, passWord);
Connection   *conn2   =   connPool->createConnection
(username, passWord);
Connection   *conn3   =   connPool->createConnection
(username, passWord);

After this code was run, the connections I counted thru 'DBA Studio' was still 1. Does it mean that "ConnectionPool" do not create 'conn2' or 'conn3'?

✍ ANSWER

Real connections are created only when there is a roundtrip requirement. In this case, you saw one connection because that is the "minConn" of the pool, and it gets created when the pool is created. The "createConnection()" calls 'create virtual connections', and they get real connections mapped from the pool at the time of a roundtrip. The un-mapping happens as soon as the roundtrip is done. If there is a need by multiple threads concurrently for doing roundtrips, then the pool size grows to serve all the threads concurrently.

☞ QUESTION 100

OCCI multithreading prerequisites

I have an issue when executing OCCI code in multiple threads.

In each thread, I encounter the following issues:

1. I am basically doing operations like bulk inserts to global temporary tables;
2. I am getting "core dumps" when I try to commit the inserts to the GTT;
3. I am using a separate 'Connection' for each thread spawned;
4. I am using the OCCI Environment with "THREADED_ MUTEXED" mode or object;

Are there any prerequisites to be taken care of before I start out using OCCI in a multi-threaded mode?

✍ ANSWER

You can download OCCI programmer's Guide to check your needs. The information that I know of, only the 'Environment', 'Mpa', 'ConnectionPool' and 'Connection' are thread-safe. I.e. the others (Statement,ResultSet etc..) are not thread-safe.

INDEX

Attention SAP Experts

Have you ever considered writing a book in your area of SAP? Equity Press is the leading provider of knowledge products in SAP applications consulting, development, and support. If you have a manuscript or an idea of a manuscript, we'd love to help you get it published!

Please send your manuscript or manuscript ideas to jim@sapcookbook.com – we'll help you turn your dream into a reality.

Or mail your inquiries to:

Equity Press Manuscripts
BOX 706
Riverside, California
92502

Tel (951)788-0810
Fax (951)788-0812

50% Off your next
SAPCOOKBOOK order

If you plan of placing an order for 10 or more books from www.sapcookbook.com you qualify for volume discounts. Please send an email to books@sapcookbook.com or phone 951-788-0810 to place your order.

You can also fax your orders to 951-788-0812 .

Interview books are great for cross-training

In the new global economy, the more you know the better. The sharpest consultants are doing everything they can to pick up more than one functional area of SAP. Each of the following Certification Review / Interview Question books provides an excellent starting point for your module learning and investigation. These books get you started like no other book can – by providing you the information that you really need to know, and fast.

SAPCOOKBOOK Interview Questions, Answers, and Explanations

ABAP	-	SAP ABAP Certification Review: SAP ABAP Interview Questions, Answers, and Explanations
SD	-	SAP SD Interview Questions, Answers, and Explanations
Security	-	SAP Security: SAP Security Essentials
HR	-	mySAP HR Interview Questions, Answers, and Explanations: SAP HR Certification Review
BW	-	SAP BW Ultimate Interview Questions, Answers, and Explanations: SAW BW Certification Review
	-	SAP SRM Interview Questions Answers and Explanations
Basis	-	SAP Basis Certification Questions: Basis Interview Questions, Answers, and Explanations
MM	-	SAP MM Certification and Interview Questions: SAP MM Interview Questions, Answers, and Explanations

SAP BW Ultimate Interview Questions, Answers, and Explanations

Key Topics Include:

- The most important BW settings to know
- BW tables and transaction code quick references
- Certification Examination Questions
- Extraction, Modeling and Configuration
- Transformations and Administration
- Performance Tuning, Tips & Tricks, and FAQ
- Everything a BW resource needs to know before an interview

mySAP HR Interview Questions, Answers, and Explanations

Key topics include:

- The most important HR settings to know
- mySAP HR Administration tables and transaction code quick references
- SAP HR Certification Examination Questions
- Org plan, Compensation, Year End, Wages, and Taxes
- User Management, Transport System, Patches, and Upgrades
- Benefits, Holidays, Payroll, and Infotypes
- Everything an HR resource needs to know before an interview

SAP SRM Interview Questions, Answers, and Explanations

Key Topics Include:

- The most important SRM Configuration to know
- Common EBP Implementation Scenarios
- Purchasing Document Approval Processes
- Supplier Self Registration and Self Service (SUS)
- Live Auctions and Bidding Engine, RFX Processes (LAC)
- Details for Business Intelligence and Spend Analysis
- EBP Technical and Troubleshooting Information

SAP MM Interview Questions, Answers, and Explanations

- The most important MM Configuration to know
- Common MM Implementation Scenarios
- MM Certification Exam Questions
- Consumption Based Planning
- Warehouse Management
- Material Master Creation and Planning
- Purchasing Document Inforecords

SAP SD Interview Questions, Answers, and Explanations

- The most important SD settings to know
- SAP SD administration tables and transaction code quick references
- SAP SD Certification Examination Questions
- Sales Organization and Document Flow Introduction
- Partner Procedures, Backorder Processing, Sales BOM
- Backorder Processing, Third Party Ordering, Rebates and Refunds
- Everything an SD resource needs to know before an interview

SAP Basis Interview Questions, Answers, and Explanations

- The most important Basis settings to know
- Basis Administration tables and transaction code quick references
- Certification Examination Questions
- Oracle database, UNIX, and MS Windows Technical Information
- User Management, Transport System, Patches, and Upgrades
- Backup and Restore, Archiving, Disaster Recover, and Security
- Everything a Basis resource needs to know before an interview

SAP Security Essentials

- Finding Audit Critical Combinations
- Authentication, Transaction Logging, and Passwords
- Roles, Profiles, and User Management
- ITAR, DCAA, DCMA, and Audit Requirements
- The most important security settings to know
- Security Tuning, Tips & Tricks, and FAQ
- Transaction code list and table name references

SAP Workflow Interview Questions, Answers, and Explanations

- Database Updates and Changing the Standard
- List Processing, Internal Tables, and ALV Grid Control
- Dialog Programming, ABAP Objects
- Data Transfer, Basis Administration
- ABAP Development reference updated for 2006!
- Everything an ABAP resource needs to know before an interview

Lightning Source UK Ltd.
Milton Keynes UK
08 April 2010

152497UK00001B/172/A